THE GOSPEL OF

John

William R. Cannon

THE UPPER ROOM
Nashville, Tennessee

The Gospel of John

Scripture quotations not otherwise identified are from the authorized King James Version of the Bible.

Scripture quotations designated RSV are from the Revised Standard Version of the Bible, copyrighted 1946, 1952, and © 1971 by the Division of Christian Education, National Council of the Churches of Christ in the United States of America, and are used by permission.

Scripture quotations designated AP are the author's paraphrase.

Book design: Harriette Bateman
First printing: May 1985 (7)
Library of Congress Catalog Card Number: 84-052230
ISBN 0-8358-0511-5
Printed in the United States of America

THE GOSPEL OF JOHN

CONTENTS

Preface 7

Introduction 9

1. The Prologue *John 1:1–14* 13

2. The Incarnate Word *John 1:15–4:54* 17

3. The Incarnate Deed *John 5:1–8:11* 35

4. The Incarnate Light *John 8:12–10:21* 49

5. The Incarnate Life *John 10:22–11:57* 59

6. The Incarnate Way *John 12:1–13:38* 71

7. The Incarnate Truth *John 14:1–17:26* 83

8. The Incarnate God *John 18:1–20:31* 95

9. The Epilogue *John 21:1–25* 113

Questions for Reflection and Study 117

PREFACE

THIS BOOK ON the Gospel of John brings to completion my commentaries on the four Gospels. I began, when Dr. Wilson Weldon was World Editor of The Upper Room, by writing *A Disciple's Profile of Jesus*. It is a study of the Gospel of Luke. Dr. Weldon's successor, Dr. Maxie Dunnam, a former student of mine, encouraged me to write *Jesus the Servant,* a study of Mark, and also the *Gospel of Matthew.* Now Dr. Rueben Job has invited me to do this fourth book on John.

In my mind, the other three were preparation for this fourth one. Since I first began to read the Bible (I read it in its entirety when I was nine years old), John's Gospel has been my favorite book. Next to our Lord himself, the Apostle John has been my favorite character in the New Testament. So the writing of this book, from start to finish, has been a labor of love.

It is not possible to indicate the books that have guided me in its preparation. If I take into account indirect influences, books that I have read on the subject over the years but to which I have not referred in my actual writing, the number would be too numerous to recall. My resources were almost as comprehensive as the material about Jesus mentioned by the author of the Fourth Gospel himself (John 21:25). But if I take into account direct influences, books I have referred to in preparation of the manuscript, the number would be embarrassingly few.

To tell the truth, I have written this book with mainly the Gospel of John itself before me. To be sure, the study will offer sound instruction on the Gospel, I trust, to the reader.

But its purpose is to edify as well as to enlighten. It is written to appeal to the heart as well as the mind.

I am indebted to Ms. Janice Grana for encouragement in its preparation and to her coworkers in editing the manuscript and preparing the study questions on each chapter. I am most grateful to my secretary, Mrs. Vivian Mitchell, for typing and retyping the drafts, especially since I have written it all in longhand and my handwriting is poor.

WILLIAM R. CANNON
RALEIGH, NORTH CAROLINA
PENTECOST SEASON, 1984

INTRODUCTION

THE ASSUMPTION FOR a long time was that the first three Gospels—Matthew, Mark, and Luke—are factual accounts of the life of Jesus; while the Fourth Gospel—John—is less concerned with the earthly life but more concerned with reflecting on the career of Jesus. As early as the third century, John was called "the spiritual Gospel."

The assumption is no longer valid. Every one of the Gospels is written from a theological perspective. The materials presented in all four are arranged thematically—not just chronologically.

Their arrangement is to delineate the points of view of the various authors. Prophecy was dear to Matthew. He saw Jesus as the fulfillment of the messianic promises of God in the Old Testament. Mark was an activist and a conscientious Jew. To him Jesus was the busy Servant of God, working in behalf of God's chosen people, the Jews, doing everything he could to save them from their sins. Luke was a missionary, and his mission as the companion to Paul was to the Gentiles. To him, Jesus was the universal person, the one who brought the grace and favor of God to the whole of humanity.

John's perspective is different still. He was a mystic, or, at least, the mystical elements in his nature were more pronounced than in the nature of the other three evangelists. He saw Jesus, not so much as he appeared to be from the outward aspects of his ministry, as he did from the basic purpose that ministry was designed to achieve. All four writers, to be sure, deduced their theological concepts from the activity and teaching of Jesus. Even though the other three found room within history to display their meaning, John saw the work of Jesus as so comprehensive and stupendous that his mission defied the bounds of history and was commensurate with eternity itself. John saw Jesus, not as the agent of God, but as God himself. For him the Redeemer and Creator are one and the same. So he wrote a Gospel that portrays Jesus as the incarnate God.

All the evangelists report facts, and the facts in John's Gospel are just as reliable as those in Matthew's, Mark's, and Luke's. John was no more a novelist than any of the rest. There is no fiction whatever in the four Gospels. What they relate actually took place. Jesus did what they say he did!

Though the Gospels are not novels, they are not biographies either. None, not even Mark, sets out to write a full account of the life of Jesus. These authors were evangelists. They used their materials selectively in order to convince their readers that salvation comes through Jesus Christ and through him alone. They describe exactly what took place, but their purpose in describing what took place is to show their readers why these incidents took place and their crucial relevance for them. John is very explicit in giving the reason he wrote his Gospel: "that ye might believe that Jesus is the Christ, the Son of God; and that believing ye might have life through his name" (20:31).

Do not assume, therefore, that John was a theologian, while the other three evangelists were historians without any theological predilections at all. They were all theologians who based their theology on the life and teachings of Jesus. But John was a more profound and more discerning theologian than the other three. He employed thought patterns in vogue in the secular philosophies of his day in order to elucidate his concepts of Jesus. Therefore, antiquity ascribed to him and him alone the title, "the Theologian." Antiquity did not confer this title even on Paul, who shared with John the task of forming Christian theology. "Theologian," as it refers to the author of the Fourth Gospel, is both a title and an endearing nickname. Its purpose is to concede to him first place among all the theologians of Christendom. His Christology has never been matched, much less excelled.

Who was this remarkable man, and when and where did he live? There are two ways of answering these questions. One is to seek clues within the Gospel itself. The other is to look for external evidence—that is, the testimony of contemporaries or near contemporaries familiar with the book and presumably with the circumstances of its origin. Recent scholarship has centered almost entirely on the first, focusing its attention on the Gospel, its style, ideas, and social milieu. Research, of course, has been familiar with external evidence but has largely discounted it by calling it inconsistent with the contents of the Gospel itself. For example, it has contended that the ideas expressed in John are too late in time for it to have been written in the first or early second century and so could not have been composed by an apostle or contemporary of Jesus. It is more Hellenistic than Judaistic. It appears to belong to the culture of the Roman Empire rather than to the traditions of a conquered province along the Jordan River, hovering between Egypt and Mesopotamia. But, due to the discovery of the Dead Sea Scrolls, we know that the same ideas were in circulation in Jesus' time and right at home in the land where he and his disciples lived. The geographical information in John is more extensive and more accurate than that of any of the other Gospels. There are more personal references in it than elsewhere.

Note that nothing whatever in the Gospel precludes its having been written by a Jew and a contemporary of Jesus. Also there is much to indicate that the author knew his hero personally and must have been with him for much that he did. The reader may reasonably assume, therefore, that the traditional outside evidence as to authorship and plan of composition is reliable and true.

Irenaeus, who wrote around A.D. 180, ascribes the authorship of the Fourth Gospel to the Apostle John. He also affirms that he studied under Polycarp, who, in turn, studied under John. Likewise, Ephesus is designated as the abode of John, who was its bishop, and as the city where he wrote his Gospel. Eusebius, the first historian of Christianity after Luke (who wrote the Acts of the Apostles), states that after the three Gospels of Matthew, Mark, and Luke had been written, the Apostle John read them and attested to their truth. He said, however, they lacked an account of what Christ did in his early ministry prior to the arrest of John the Baptist. According to Eusebius, John wrote his Gospel to compensate for this deficiency. If that be the case, John must have been written in Ephesus either during the last decade of the first century or the first decade of the second century. The Gospel, then, is the account of an eyewitness, a person privy to the thoughts and feelings of Jesus, and one of his dearest friends. He could join the other disciples, as they could join him, in saying, "That which was from the beginning...which we have looked upon, and our hands have handled, of the Word of life" (1 John 1:1) is the burden of our testimony and the contents of this Gospel.

CHAPTER ONE

THE PROLOGUE

John 1:1–14

GOSPEL MEANS "GOOD NEWS." In the prologue to his Gospel, John announces the good news and tells both from whom it comes and to whom it is sent. Most important of all, he identifies the messenger who brings it. The startling information he gives is *the message and the messenger are one and the same*. The Word God sends is the person of his own dear son.

Paul is the apostle of the crucifixion, teaching us that our salvation rests on the atonement, that Christ by his death on the cross made restitution for the sins of the whole world. John, however, is the apostle of the incarnation, teaching us that God became human in order that we might know him, come to love him, and by his grace be made like him, so that we, too, might become divine. In Jesus, the Word of the Father appeared for the first time in the flesh of humanity.

In the Book of Genesis, creation is described in terms of speech. God uttered his voice, and the words he spoke became creative acts. God said, "Let there be light: and there was light" (Gen. 1:3). God said that there should be day and night, evening and morning, heaven and earth, land and sea, sun and moon, vegetables and animals, and, finally, man and woman (Gen. 1:5–27). Whatever God said came to be. John tells us that this same creative Word which was with God from the beginning, and was indeed basic to God's nature, has now become a creature, a specific human being, so that we are able to see the Creator in a form of his creation. The infinite has expressed itself in the finite. The eternal has been poured into a temporal event. And the divine has been

13

personified in the human. Indeed, God himself has become human.

Stoicism was a popular philosophy at the time of John. It conceived of God in terms of mind (pure thought). *Logos,* which we translate as *Word,* is the Stoic name for the mind of God. God pervades the universe in its entirety and to a certain extent is synonymous with it. But God's special habitation is in the human mind, and the duty of a person is to live in accord with the Logos (God). Philo of Alexandria, who lived from 13 B.C. to A.D. 50, approximately, and who used Stoic philosophy in his interpretation of the Old Testament and adapted it to his own purposes to such a degree that he might be called a Jewish Stoic, obviously had considerable influence on the author of the Gospel of John. According to Philo, the Logos dwelt in the minds of Moses and the prophets and gave them their inspiration. But the Logos dwelt in them only intermittently. It came and went. When they were inspired and uttered divine truth, the Logos was in them. Then, it could be said, they possessed the Logos. But often they were without the Logos and functioned on their own as mere creatures. But John teaches that the Logos, or divine Word, never left Jesus; Jesus was that Word. What was only intermittent in the heroes of the Old Testament was constant and permanent in Jesus Christ.

Shakespeare got ideas and suggestion from the histories of England and writings contemporary with him and transformed them into his plays, which are masterpieces of the English language. Similarly, John used Philo to advantage and borrowed a philosophical teaching from him which John, by the inspiration of the Holy Spirit and his own genius, translated into christological theology unmatched in all the literature of the world.

A child in school gets some knowledge from his or her textbook, but often not enough to comprehend the subject with which the textbook deals. The child's teacher who provides personal instruction comes to personify for the child the subject and makes the contents of the textbook come alive so that the pupil is able thoroughly to learn it. According to

John, the writings of the Old Testament are God's textbook; but Jesus Christ is the teacher who brings to life the truth which the Old Testament contains.

Platonic philosophy teaches that what we see and experience in this world is but a copy or crude imitation of perfect forms or ideas that can never be concretized. But with John, perfection has been concretized in the Word made flesh. The crude copy has been displayed as the ideal reality in Jesus Christ. Although Matthew and Luke begin their Gospels with the human ancestry and birth of Jesus of Nazareth, John begins his with Christ in his preexistent state, with him as he was with the Father through all eternity. In this regard, John's Gospel is preliminary to the synoptic Gospels and essential to their understanding. The Fourth Gospel declares the incarnation, that the divine Word was personified and that the son of God became man. The first and third Gospels tell how this came about, that the son of God on earth was conceived in the womb of a woman and that God entered history through birth as the child of Mary. John does not contradict Matthew and Luke. Rather he enunciates the theological principle that makes the historical fact of the birth of Jesus as they describe it both understandable and necessary.

There are four basic truths enunciated in this prologue. The first truth is that the Word has always been with God as a distinct entity or being. There never was a time when the Word did not exist. And there is no qualitative difference between the Word and God, for the Word was and is God. Therefore, the germinal seed of the doctrine of the Trinity is supplied by John. It is he who plants it in the first topsoil of Christianity. The Word (son) preexists with the Father (1:1–2), and he shares equally with God the Father in all his activity (1:3).

The second truth is that the eternal mission of the Word is to enable people to have life by believing in him (1:4,7). This is the sole purpose of the incarnation of the Word. *Life,* as John uses that word in the prologue, is not mere existence. If it meant no more than existence, everyone who is alive has that anyway; and there is no need for the mission of the

Word. *Life,* as John uses that word, is a quality of existence that makes the recipient like God. That qualitative life has permanent quality. It exists forever. It never ends.

The third truth is that the result of the mission of the Word is problematical. That mission is both successful and unsuccessful, depending upon the response it evokes. Some people receive the Word. But others do not. Only those who freely receive the Word of God are given the power to become the children of God (1:11–13). Others stay as they are. Those who believe and open their hearts to the Word become like God.

The fourth truth, which is basic to the other three, is that incarnation is a historical fact, that the Word became a definite person, a real identifiable human being, whom believers recognized as possessing divine characteristics. The climax of the prologue is its last verse: "And the Word was made flesh, and dwelt among us, (and we beheld his glory, the glory as of the only begotten of the Father,) full of grace and truth" (1:14).

CHAPTER TWO

THE INCARNATE WORD

John 1:15–4:54

IN THIS FIRST section of the Gospel after the prologue, the Apostle John displays the Word in a series of incidents and encounters that Jesus had at the outset of his ministry. By the incarnation, God reveals his purpose. The divine Word is spoken through the calling of the first disciples, in Jesus' manifestation of his own nature at Cana, and especially in the all-inclusiveness of his message as he proclaims it to the Jews, the Samaritans, and the gentiles.

The Herald and the Disciples (1:15–51)

Though John the Baptist is introduced as the herald of the Word in the prologue itself (1:6–7), who John was and the manner in which he performed are presented immediately following the prologue in a separate section of the Gospel. Here the emphasis is on witness. And the center of attention is John the Baptist, who was the herald, the first witness, to the incarnate Word.

The descriptive label, "the Baptist," which is now invariably attached to John the forerunner of Jesus, arises from the fact that John baptized Jesus in the River Jordan and thereby inaugurated him for his mission. But this title is an imposition on the herald as he is presented in the Fourth Gospel. Though Matthew and Mark both describe the baptism of Jesus by John (Matt. 3:13–17; Mark 1:9–11) and though Luke omits the description but nonetheless implies the event (Luke 3:21), the author of the Fourth Gospel does neither. From reading John, one would never know that Jesus had been baptized at all.

Indeed, the herald's own work, as a baptizer of others who came to him on the banks of the Jordan, is almost unnoticed in this Gospel. It is mentioned only incidentally and by critics who ask him what right he has to baptize (1:25). The Baptist's reply is casual and to the point of being almost self-degrading and ultimately unimportant. For he says, "I just use water. That is all. Maybe it does some good. But real baptism is yet to come. My main mission is something else. I am here to point out another much greater than myself and whose work will be far superior to mine" (1:26–27, AP).

The truth of the matter is that we would not be able to know what it was John the Baptist was doing on the banks of the Jordan before he announced the Word if it were not for the synoptic Gospels. We would be mystified as to his activity and bewildered as to why the Jews sent priests and levites from Jerusalem to observe him and to inquire about his mission (1:19). It is from the synoptics that we learn that he preached judgment and repentance and that he baptized ones who confessed their sins. John omits all this. Evidently, he presupposes on the part of his readers a knowledge of the first three Gospels. His one concern is to announce the presence of the incarnate Word. He is indifferent to anything else.

Although Matthew and Mark describe the Baptist in a fierce and rugged manner, clothed in camel's hair and with a belt of skin, eating locusts and wild honey, John does not describe him at all. Even though the authors of the first two Gospels picture him as if he were Elijah come back to earth again, the author of the Fourth Gospel reports that the Baptist disclaims any connection with Elijah (1:21).

The herald is content to be only a herald. John the Baptist does not want to get in the way of what he is commissioned to do. He does not want the sign to obstruct that to which it points. The synoptics stress baptism, even to the point that Jesus submitted to it, though he was without sin and really did not need it. He submitted to baptism in order to set a good example for others and to impress upon them that they should accept baptism and repentance for the remission of their sins. Indeed, that is what Matthew, Mark, and Luke imply in their accounts of the baptism of Jesus. But John has a higher and wider vision. The act of baptism is incidental to what should take place through baptism. True baptism is not just the sprinkling with, dipping in, or pouring on water. True baptism is the infusion of the Holy Spirit. John points away from the mechanical act of baptism to the incarnate Word of God, who alone can baptize the believer with his own spirit and infuse into him or her the power of everlasting life. "And of his fullness have all we received, and grace for grace" (1:16).

Jesus Christ supersedes Moses, who, as God's lawgiver, could only issue commands and prohibitions, so that the burden of responsibility lay on the people to obey his edicts. Jesus Christ brought grace, the undeserved mercy of God, and truth, the living Word of God, which not only showed people what righteousness is but also provided them with the means of attaining it. What was once an ominous obligation is now a joyous privilege. Frightful responsibility has been replaced by creative opportunity (1:17).

The Baptist freely admits that he whom he announces stands before him in time as well as honor (1:15). Jesus Christ comes from "the bosom of the Father" (1:18), that is, he possesses God's heart as well as his mind. Since no one has ever seen God, we are dependent entirely upon his only begotten son for our knowledge and understanding of him. All the herald can do is prepare the way for Christ's coming and point him out when he arrives (1:23, 29). The contrast between the forerunner and his Lord is so great that John the Baptist feels unworthy to unlace the sandals on Jesus' feet (1:27). This was a task performed by a household slave. John in relationship to Jesus is less than a slave in relationship to his owner. Such is the Baptist's estimate of himself as given in his response to the inquiry of the Pharisees from Jerusalem.

This dialogue between John the Baptist and these Jewish emissaries took place on one day. The author of the Fourth Gospel is the only one of the Gospel writers to give the exact location of John's baptism, namely "Bethabara" (1:28), on the east side of the Jordan River, which today is in Jordan

near the Dead Sea. This was a definite site in the wilderness
of Judea.

The next day Jesus made his appearance, and John the
Baptist recognized him and pointed him out to the crowd
gathered on the banks of the river. Though John and Jesus
were cousins, John had possibly never seen Jesus before. As
Jesus arrived, John saw a dove fly down from heaven and
light upon him and remain on him. He knew this to symbolize the descent of the Holy Spirit, God's identification of his
only begotten son (1:31–34). This enabled John to make the
dramatic announcement: "Behold the Lamb of God, which
taketh away the sin of the world" (1:29).

This announcement is the sum and substance of the
Baptist's mission, the very reason for his life. It is also a
précis of Jesus' own ministry of redemption. It brings to
glorious fulfillment all the promises of the Old Testament.
Here in Jesus is the paschal lamb of the Passover in Egypt,
when the firstborn of the Jews were spared and those of the
Egyptians killed (Exod. 12). Here is the goat of the atonement sent away into the wilderness with the sins of the
Jewish people upon him (Lev. 16:21 ff). Here is the sacrificial
lamb offered daily on the altar of the Temple. Here is the
lamb as the suffering servant (see Isa. 53:7), who is a
subsitute for the transgressions of God's people. Here is also
the new covenant in Christ's blood, by which all humanity
can be redeemed and which gives to the world the conquering
lamb who is victorious over all evil and is the ruler of God's
people. This is John's announcement of the Messiah.

On the third day in the same place, John pointed Jesus
out, as he walked through the crowd, to two of his own
disciples, who heard him speak and were so fascinated by
him that they walked behind him after he had finished his
discourse and was leaving the people. Jesus noticed them,
stopped, and asked them what they wanted. Embarrassed,
they replied, "Teacher, where do you live?"

"Why don't you come and see?" Jesus said smiling.
The two accepted his invitation. The time was four o'clock in
the afternoon, the tenth hour of the Hebrew day, which ended
at sunset. Presumably they spent the night with him. One of
them was Andrew, who gave his impression of Jesus to his

brother Simon; and Simon went with him to see Andrew's new master. The author of the Fourth Gospel tells us that immediately on seeing Simon, Jesus gave him the nickname "Cephas" or "Peter", which means "stone" or "rock" (1:42). This encounter of Peter with Jesus had to happen on the fourth day, since there would not have been time enough between four o'clock and sunset for Andrew to go for his brother and bring him back to Jesus.

Thus it was on the fourth day that Jesus left the wilderness of Judea and went back home into Galilee. There he found Philip, a fellow townsman of Andrew and Peter, from Bethsaida, which is near Capernaum on the banks of the Sea of Galilee. Jesus said to Philip, "Follow me," and he did. Then Philip told his brother Nathanael about Jesus, saying that he and their friends, Andrew and Simon, had found him about whom Moses and the prophets had written, and that he was Jesus, the son of Joseph of Nazareth. Nathanael skeptically replied, "Can any good thing come out of Nazareth?" Nazareth was so inconsequential a place that it had not been mentioned in the Hebrew Bible.

"Well, at least come and meet him," Philip said. "Then you will see for yourself."

And indeed Nathanael did see. He was amazed when Jesus told him that before Philip reached him, Jesus had seen Nathanael clearly sitting under a fig tree. This was all the skeptic needed to be convinced. He believed and became a disciple. Jesus said, "Nathanel, it did not take much to convince you. You haven't seen anything yet. There will come a time when you will see the heavens open and angels ascending and descending on me." In the imagery of Jacob's dream, Jesus implied that he himself was the ladder to heaven.

This, as given in the Gospel of John, is the manner in which the first five disciples were chosen, yet we know the names of only four of them: Andrew, Simon (Peter), Philip, and Nathanael. Who was that unidentified disciple who with Andrew first followed Jesus? No doubt, it was John himself. The author of the Fourth Gospel was too modest to write his own name.

These first five were all Galileans. Three of them,

however, were chosen in Judea either at or near the site of John the Baptist's mission. Two were chosen in Galilee itself. We know four of them came from Bethsaida, and probably the fifth did as well. They were all friends of one another. There is no question but that they had all been disciples of John the Baptist; so they had been prepared in advance by the herald for him of whom the herald spoke. This means that before the Messiah could begin his messianic mission, he had to have disciples to help him perform it. Just as in the beginning, the utterance of God's Word made the universe and its inhabitants; so now the sending of God's Word to earth immediately made disciples. The Word spoken is also the Word heard. At least five persons besides John the Baptist believed.

The First Miracle and the First Confrontation with the Jews (2:1–25)

Although the three synoptics follow the baptism of Jesus by John the Baptist with his temptation by the devil, John follows the acknowledgement of Jesus by the Baptist and the selection of the first disciples with the performance of his first miracle at Cana of Galilee. Indeed, John does not report the temptation at all. The first three Gospels emphasize the humanity of Jesus. The Fourth Gospel declares his divinity. It was there in the Galilean village of Cana that Jesus first "manifested forth his glory" (2:11). There the incarnate Word publicly expressed the power of deity.

According to John, three days after the conversation with Nathanael, Jesus and his disciples accepted an invitation to the wedding of a friend. Though John recounts the calling of only five of the disciples, probably the other seven had been constituted as well. The evangelist chose to deal selectively with the event, focusing attention on those of Bethsaida alone, simply because they had been friends of John the Baptist before any of them met Jesus. Chances are, all twelve disciples were with Jesus at the wedding. Otherwise, John would have said that Jesus went to Cana with some or a few of his disciples. By saying "the disciples," he implies that all of them accompanied him to the wedding. They were there because of Jesus. And Jesus was there because of his mother.

Certainly he was reluctant to perform a miracle. The wedding was hardly the place to do what he did. And what he did seems inconsequential in comparison with his power and the divine glory that power displayed. Think of the inestimable human need about him. Think of all the wrongs crying to be righted, all the pain needing relief, all the illnesses requiring cures, all the evil that ought to be conquered and destroyed, all the sins that should be forgiven and obliterated, even life itself struggling against death and needing his divine intervention to survive. But all he did was turn water into wine. He, thereby, relieved the embarrassment of a host who had run out of refreshments for his guests. Why would Jesus perform a miracle to satisfy the thirst for wine of guests who may have had too much to drink already? Even the place where the miracle was performed was restricted and circumscribed, even segregated, if we may use that word without implying racial discrimination. What place is more private than a wedding? People come there only by invitation, and the general public is excluded.

Nonetheless, Jesus performed this miracle. And it was the first one that he did perform. Why? Because sickness, injury, pain, poverty, and dissatisfaction are the exceptions to life, not its general characteristics. Jesus would deal with all those in due time. Evil, taught Augustine, is the deprivation of good. There could be no evil if first there were no good. It is a serious mistake to limit the Gospel to the poor, the underprivileged, and the dispossessed. The religion of Jesus Christ is for everybody. So the first miracle was performed for those who from a superficial point of view did not need a miracle. They would have been just as well off without the wine as with it. But they expected it, and Jesus saw to it that their expectations were not disappointed.

God is not someone we call on to help us only when we can't help ourselves. The wine was something people could provide for themselves. It was either the short-sightedness of the host or the inordinate appetite of the guests that caused the shortage at the wedding. Bonhoeffer correctly observed that if God's purpose in our lives is merely to give us what we cannot get elsewhere, then as technology improves and science discovers more and more, our need for God will decrease proportionately. In this regard, the secular is always encroaching on the sacred.

But Jesus teaches a deeper lesson through this miracle that God is present in every aspect of life. He intensifies our joy and excitement in the pleasant experiences of life, as well as comforts and sustains us in times of distress and grief. The first miracle took place at a party, not in either the synagogue or the Temple.

It is interesting to observe that Jesus used the six waterpots Jews used for washing their arms and purifying themselves before a feast. In other words, he took sacred objects to provide people with secular pleasure. But then, he knew, and he wanted others to realize, that the sacred exists for the secular, that religion is charged to provide its devotees every day with the fullness of life.

In the Jewish society of the first century, the ruler of the feast was one of the guests chosen from among all those invited to the wedding to be the toastmaster and to express well wishes to the nuptial pair. The toastmaster was surprised that the best wine was served last. Ordinarily, the good wine came first. Later on, as the guests indulged themselves, they would become less aware of the inferior quality of what they were drinking. But due to the miracle, the best wine came last. So in life, the quality of our living is constantly enhanced and made more satisfying by every new experience we have with God. The more conscious we become of God's presence, the more we realize the joy and fulfillment of being alive. This first miracle teaches us that happiness is the purpose of God for everybody, but happiness that is genuine and enduring cannot be had except from the hands of God. We cannot give it to ourselves.

After only an interval of a few days with his mother and brothers in Capernaum, Jesus and his disciples went to Jerusalem to keep the feast of the Passover. Though both John and the synoptics have Jesus begin his ministry in

Galilee, John's presentation of the master's stay in Galilee is brief. The synoptics indicate that the greater part of our Lord's ministry was spent in Galilee and only the last week of it in Jerusalem. John, in contrast, has Jesus going back and forth from the capital to his home province of Galilee.

Likewise, the synoptics place the cleansing of the Temple during Holy Week after Jesus' triumphal entry into Jerusalem, while John puts it on the Passover following Jesus' first miracle in Cana. This is because all four evangelists arrange incidents topically rather than chronologically. The placing suits the theological emphasis each is attempting to make.

There are more details in the Johannine account of the cleansing than in any of the synoptics. John describes the whip or "scourge" Jesus used to drive out the money-changers and the merchants (2:15). It was a whip made of cords, such as was used to drive cattle in that day. John tells us that the merchants were selling "oxen and sheep" as well as pigeons (2:14). Like the synoptics, John recalls Jesus' protest against making God's house a market for trade. The disciples recall one of the messianic psalms, where it is written: "Zeal for thy house will consume me" (2:17, RSV; also Psalm 69:9).

But the similarity between John's account and the accounts of the synoptics stops at this point. John focuses on the conversation between Jesus and the Jews. In John, the Jews are interested only in a sign, some divine corroboration for Jesus' actions. Could he demonstrate the legitimacy for his actions by performing a miracle? In other words, they are not indignant over his driving out the merchants and money-changers. Even they perhaps are doubtful that it is proper to conduct such business in God's house. But they want to be sure, and the only way they can be sure that Jesus is doing what ought to be done is for him to convince them with a miracle. And Jesus does not dispute their right to make this claim on him. He is willing for his act to be subject to verification. But he puts the verification for what he has done in the future. "Tear the Temple down," he says, "and I will rebuild it in three days" (2:19, AP).

This is incredible. The Temple at that time was still unfinished, and Herod and his followers had been working on it for forty-six years. But Jesus did not mean Herod's Temple. He meant the temple of his own body. Without the Jews' knowing it, he had struck at the roots of their religion. God's temple is the devout and sincere worshiper, not a building made by hands. Jesus had driven out the money-changers, because God does not demand Jewish currency for the purchase of his sacrifice. Foreign coins were unacceptable in Temple worship. Proselytes and Jews from abroad had to exchange the valuable Roman currency into the cheap currency of the province before they could buy a sacrifice to offer God. But then God did not, in Jesus' opinion, want any ceremonial sacrifice anyway. He wanted the heart and life of the worshiper. Worship is not just for the Jews. Worship is for anyone who believes. Jesus thought it was wrong to exclude the gentiles from the inner court of the Temple. God's house shall be a house for all nations, yet if gentiles went beyond the Court of the Gentiles, the Jews would put them to death.

Jesus performed miracles in Jerusalem. As a result, many believed. Yet our Lord took no satisfaction from human testimony in his favor. He knew human nature, and he realized how fickle it is (2:23–25). His confidence was in himself.

The Word Spoken to the Jews (3:1–36)

Jesus' confidence was in himself, and in himself alone, because he knew that he was the manifestation of the Father. As God's Incarnate Word, his first obligation was to manifest himself to his own people, that is, to speak God's word to the Jews. The author of the Fourth Gospel depicts Jesus' doing this in his conversation with Nicodemus (3:1–21); and he confirms the validity of Jesus' action in his account of the last testimony of John the Baptist to the mission of Jesus (3:22–36). Our Lord told Nicodemus what the Jews must believe in order to be saved (3:18). And John the Baptist testifies that God sent Jesus, and, therefore, whatever Jesus says is a message brought directly from God (3:34).

Nicodemus is identified as a ruler of the Jews. This means that since he was a Jew and not a Roman, he was an active member of the Sanhedrin, the governing body of Jewry under the Roman procurator. The policy of Rome was to allow the peoples of its conquered provinces a certain measure of local autonomy. Rome did not destroy national institutions and traditions but rather employed them to its own imperial purposes and designs. The Sanhedrin was a body of priests and scribes presided over by the high priest. Since Israel and Judah had always been theocratic states with God as their supreme ruler, the priests even under the monarchy had exercised great power in the kingdom. After the exile, when there were no kings, their power had increased. Indeed, during the period of Hasmonean independence, the priests had been the titled rulers of the land. Therefore Rome permitted the Sanhedrin to make most decisions. This saved her the bother of constant adjudication among a naturally quarrelsome and disgruntled people. In the Jewish mind, there was no distinction between the secular and the sacred anyway; so every decision the Sanhedrin made was ultimately a religious one. Nicodemus was a worthy member of that august body.

Oddly enough, this Jew has a Greek name, indicating a Hellenistic background. His family must have been of the diaspora, that is, Jews who lived abroad and only occasionally came back to the homeland to observe the Feast of the Passover. But Nicodemus himself resided permanently in Jerusalem, else he could not have been a member of the Sanhedrin. Herod the Great, in order to gain control over the Sanhedrin, would import important personages from the diaspora and place them on the Sanhedrin. There was always fierce rivalry and antagonism between these foreign leaders and the native leaders. Perhaps Nicodemus was a Herodian implant.

His name means conqueror. This is ironic, for this one who rules others came to Jesus to seek rule over himself.

He was embarrassed to come. Here he was, a prominent and well-known teacher in Israel, seeking to be taught by another, one with no official status, a controversial figure whom Nicodemus's own colleagues had come to despise. Yet what he had heard about Jesus had led Nicodemus to him. He came by night in order to escape detection. He admitted Jesus had come from God, or else he would not have been able to do what he was doing.

Jesus told Nicodemus that he *had* to be born again. As his mother had once given him physical birth, so now God must give him spiritual birth. Like the wind, this new birth appears to one out of nowhere. It takes its own direction. One cannot detect its antecedents, nor can one predict its future outcome. The new birth is the endowment of and empowerment by the Holy Spirit. All the teachings of Israel, personified by Nicodemus, are not capable of comprehending the meaning and import of the new birth (3:10).

Indeed, that is why Jesus was at that time where he was, namely to disclose to his people who live on earth heavenly things. These can be disclosed only by one who has already been in God's presence and heard those words himself. Nicodemus cannot give himself a new birth. He is correct in assuming that he cannot enter into his mother's womb a second time. He must personally believe on Jesus and accept in his heart the truth of his message. That message is simply this: "For God so loved the world, that he gave his only begotten Son, that whosoever believeth in him should not perish, but have everlasting life" (3:16). That is the essence of the gospel. That is the Word spoken by God in Jesus for all humankind to hear.

The lessons Jesus teaches through his conversation with Nicodemus are:

1. Every person must experience a spiritual birth comparable to his or her physical birth. There must come a time in a person's life when that person surrenders the control of himself or herself entirely to God. Self-control is displaced by divine control. Jesus Christ himself becomes the author of the surrendered person's new existence.

2. Likewise, the Jewish religion of which Nicodemus was an exemplary teacher requires fulfillment and perfection in Jesus Christ, who is the Messiah it has always foretold.

3. The new birth in Jesus Christ is not offered only to the Jews, but to people all over the world. The Jews are not alone God's chosen people. It is the will of God that *all* the world should be saved. Thus a Jew with a Greek name furnishes Jesus the occasion to proclaim that he is the Savior of Jew and Greek alike, indeed of the whole world.
4. The mission of Jesus is positive. He does not come as a judge to condemn but as a redeemer with the power to reclaim and transform (3:17).
5. However, for this redemption and reclamation to take place, people must be willing to accept him as truth and light, as the very Word of the Father in its final and perfect form (3:21).

God's Word spoken to the Jews is that ancestry and race, law and tradition are not enough. Exclusiveness has no place in the divine economy. Segregation is an anachronism. Salvation comes now not just to them but to them along with everybody else through Jesus Christ.

In John 3:25–30, John the Baptist confirmed the message Jesus had delivered from God to his own people. He did this, not by reference to the message, but rather to the person who delivers the message. John the Baptist's testimony was always and invariably to the messenger, not what the messenger says and does. He never departed from his divinely appointed role as herald of the Messiah.

In the synoptic Gospels, it is the Baptist himself who is dubious about Jesus and sends his disciples to gain confirmation of his authenticity. In the Fourth Gospel, it is the other way around. The Baptist's disciples, after a discussion with the Jews, ask him his studied opinion of Jesus and the validity of Jesus' ministry. In response to this inquiry, John the Baptist makes the ringing and thunderous declaration: "The Father loveth the Son, and hath given all things into his hand" (3:35). Then, having finished the mission God gave him to do and as if to dismiss himself from the stage of history, John the Baptist confesses: "He must increase, but I must decrease" (3:30). There is no more for the herald to say to the Jews. The full message of God is now being given to them in the person of God's own incarnate Word.

The Word Spoken to the Samaritans (4:1–42)

At the same time, the Word of God was also being spoken to the Samaritans, the Jews' worst enemy.

In the Fourth Gospel, the first inquiry a Jew made of Jesus came from a rabbi, learned, aristocratic, a ruler of his people; Jesus' first contact with the Samaritans was with a woman of ill repute, humble and socially unimportant, even unacceptable. She had been married five times, and the man she was now living with was not married to her. He may have had a wife and family of his own. He may have been a bachelor. But he was living with her out of wedlock.

The contrast between the two interviews is symbolic of the standing of the two races, Jewish and Samaritan. The Jews, at least in their eyes, were elitists. They were God's chosen people. The Samaritans were a mixture of races, a collection of peoples who had been herded together and returned to the land after the northern kingdom had fallen and its population deported to the land of its conqueror. The Samaritans accepted a form of the Hebrew religion. Their Bible was the Pentateuch. But they had no temple. They worshiped God on the top of Mount Gerizim.

Nicodemus, the Jew, had taken the initiative and come to Jesus. Jesus took the initiative and began conversation with this Samaritan stranger at Jacob's well at the foot of Mount Gerizim. He asked the Samaritan woman for a drink of water. This surprised her, for the Jews did not fraternize with the Samaritans. She was surprised even more, startled in fact, when Jesus said, "You should have asked me for a drink, and I would have given you living water, so that once you drink it, you would never thirst again."

"I did not ask you for a drink," she said, "because you don't even have a bucket to draw with. But where is this living water, the supply of which will do me forever? It is drudgery to come here every day to draw water from this deep well and haul it home again in a heavy jar on my head."

Jesus dropped the conversation about the water. The woman's understanding of what he had said was too materialistic and crass for him to continue this analogy. He merely said, "Bring your husband to talk to me." When she said that she had no husband, he calmly described her marital situation. This led her to realize she was talking to a prophet.

Then she tried to turn the conversation away from herself to the religious relationship between her people and the Jews. "You Jews worship God in Jerusalem," she said, "while we worship him on this mountain," pointing to Mount Gerizim.

He said, "Neither place is of any importance right now." But he reminded her that the Jews, at least, knew whom they were worshiping, while the Samaritans did not. What did he mean?

He meant that what little religion the Samaritans had they had borrowed from the Jews. To be sure, they had garbled it. Even Mount Gerizim, which was their place of worship, Moses had selected as the mountain of the blessing in contrast to its counterpart across the road, Mount Ebal, which was the mountain of the curse (Deut. 11:29; 27:12,13). "Now, however, neither Jerusalem nor Mount Gerizim holds any significance for either your people (the Samaritans)," Jesus told her, "or my people, the Jews. God can be worshiped anywhere if our heart is attuned to him and we are sincere and honest in seeking him, because God is everywhere." That is what Jesus meant when he said, "God is a Spirit: and they that worship him must worship him in spirit and in truth" (4:24).

"We will have to wait to see," the woman replied. "The Messiah will come, and he will tell us everything."

Jesus rejoined, "You won't have to wait. You have the answer now. I, to whom you are talking, am he."

The woman went to town to tell everybody everything she had heard. As she left, the disciples came, bringing food. Jesus was not hungry. He was too full of the spirit of God to want bread and meat. Harvest time could be four months off. But the harvest of souls was upon them. He wanted them to gather "fruit unto life eternal" (4:36). Though the disciples had sown no seed whatever among the Samaritans, still they had the opportunity to reap a spiritual harvest among them. It was proper for them to reap the benefits of the labors of others, if the harvest was one of human souls.

The woman brought quite a crowd from town to see

Jesus. What she said about him aroused the curiosity of the people. He stayed three days. And because of what he said to them, many of them believed on him and accepted him as their Savior.

The Word of God was not exclusively for the Jews. It was for others as well, even the Jews' worst enemy, the Samaritans. No people, no matter how devout they might claim to be, can ever possess God exclusively and use God to further their own ends. No people can make God punish their enemies. They must realize that God is not just their God, but the God of their enemies as well.

The Word Spoken to the Gentiles (4:43–54)

The Jews looked down on the Samaritans, but they were forced by political circumstances to look up to the Romans. They could avoid the Samaritans, ostracize them, segregate them, and carry on the normal affairs of life as if they did not exist. But the Jews were required every day to have dealings with the Romans, who treated them as a conquered people and managed them as a master over slaves.

The Bible student will observe in the Fourth Gospel a logical progression in God's message to all people through his son. Jesus had his first conversation with the Jews. And presumably this conversation took place in the heart of Jewry, probably in Jerusalem itself, for it was after the conversation that the fourth evangelist told us that Jesus and his disciples went out into the countryside of Judea, where John the Baptist gave his last testimony of the significance of Jesus (3:22). His second conversation, with the Samaritans, was in Samaria. Then he came to Galilee; and in Galilee, he talked with the gentiles.

Galilee was the most Hellenized of all the geographical parts of the promised land. Indeed, it was called in Jesus' time "Galilee of the Gentiles." The fourth evangelist tells us that Jesus was welcomed by the Galileans on his return from Jerusalem, for many of them had been with him at the feast in Jerusalem and had observed with appreciation and respect his behavior there. But then the evangelist reports a strange comment that Jesus himself makes, namely, that a prophet has no honor in his own country (4:44). Jesus probably did not have reference to Galilee, where he was reared, because the Galileans had received him with deference and hospitality (4:45).

The context of the statement clearly refers to where he has come from, Judea and Jerusalem, where his teaching had not been received. He is glad to have left the capital and to be back again in Galilee. Could this be the one reference in the Fourth Gospel to Jesus' birth in Bethlehem, the city of David, of the tribe of Benjamin and which gave to Judah her greatest king? If not, it means that Jesus associated citizenship with the country as a whole, not just one of its sections, and that he believed the home base of any Jewish prophet has to be in Jerusalem. This remark of his is in contrast to a similar remark he did make about Galilee in the synoptics (Mark 6:4; Matt. 13:57; Luke 4:24). This is not necessarily a contradiction. Both remarks arise out of the way Jesus is treated, and by whom, at the time he makes them. An assessment of a place can change in the light of what happens to one on any particular occasion.

An important and influential gentile, undoubtedly a Roman official, who resided in Capernaum, met Jesus in Cana and asked him to come back with him to his home to heal his son, who was desperately ill. Jesus' immediate response seemed heartless. "All you want," he said, "is to see me do some marvelous act. You won't believe me unless I perform a miracle."

The man humbly ignored the comment and the rebuke it implied. "Please, please come," he said, "or my child will die."

Jesus said, "My coming is really not necessary. Your son will not die. He will be entirely well again." The gentile took Jesus at his word. He made no further request of him.

It is important to note the difference between this contact Jesus had with the gentile and the other two with the Jew and the Samaritan. In neither of the first two contacts was there any evidence of whole-hearted acceptance of Jesus on the part of his interlocutors when the conversation began. But the gentile had heard about Jesus from others. When Jesus tested his belief by seeming to question his sincerity, the man pled with Jesus to come. Even when Jesus did not go but merely assured the man that his son would get well, the gentile accepted his word as adequate. This faith was amazing.

The Word of God did not lose its potency as it developed beyond the Old Testament. Rather it gained in effectiveness and power. Nicodemus the Jew came and found the new birth. The Samaritans asked Jesus to remain with them and help them; he tarried in Samaria three days. The Roman gentile journeyed twenty miles to find Jesus and, in finding him, had enough faith to go back alone to his home, knowing in his heart Jesus would do what he promised.

In and through God's incarnate son, the Word of the Father reached its full course. It had been spoken first to God's own chosen people, the Jews. Next, the enemies of the Jews, the Samaritans, heard it. And the gentiles, the inhabitants of the rest of the known world, received it, as well. God's Word is for all peoples. Jesus came to deliver it to the totality of humankind.

The servants of the gentile ruler met him and told him that his son's fever had subsided and the child was getting well. The father asked the time the fever had broken. He learned it was at the exact moment Jesus had told him his boy would live. "The man believed the word Jesus spoke to him" (4:50, AP).

CHAPTER THREE

THE INCARNATE DEED

John 5:1–8:11

THE WORD OF GOD is both explained and enforced by the deed of God. Jesus, in becoming God's incarnate Word to humanity, was the expression of the everlasting concern the heavenly Father has for his children. His every deed was an act of compassion and caring love. If he rebuked some, as indeed he did, it was to relieve others of mistreatment and abuse at their hands and to convince all alike that they were the children of God. This section of the Gospel is replete with acts of kindness on the part of Jesus. Each miracle is less a sign to excite wonder than it is an act of genuine service, a deed done by the son of God to benefit those in whose behalf it is performed. At the same time, each miracle is an occasion for profound theological observation on the part of the fourth evangelist, who recalls the words of Jesus himself as he testified to his relationship to God and also instructed his hearers as to their proper relationship to him as the son of God. The incarnate Deed and the incarnate Word are the same.

The Healing of a Lame Man and Its Results (5:1–47)

Because of another feast, Jesus returned to Jerusalem from Galilee. The prophet went back to the city where prophets are expected to appear, even though they are accorded no honor there. What the feast was that prompted Jesus to come, we do not know. The Jews had many feasts throughout the year. The feasts kept any devout Jew who had the leisure coming to and going from Jerusalem most of the time. A working person could afford to attend perhaps only one feast a year, if indeed any at all. A poor person might attend one or two feasts in Jerusalem in a lifetime. Since Jesus was an itinerant teacher, he, according to the Fourth Gospel, went to Jerusalem many times a year. Perhaps he attended all the feasts.

Just inside the Sheep Gate is the Pool of Bethesda. The Sheep Gate gets its name from the fact that outside it one day a week, usually Friday, shepherds gathered with their flocks to sell their animals as meat both for the table and for the Temple sacrifices.

At the Pool of Bethesda the sick and infirm gathered to seek healing. The Jews believed that at certain seasons an angel stirred the water, and the first person who stepped in while the water was bubbling was healed. One poor fellow had lain there on his pallet for thirty-eight years. He had no one to put him into the pool, and he was too lame to put himself in. Consequently, another always got ahead of him when the waters were stirred, and he missed his opportunity to be healed. There were five porches about the pool, and the lame, the sick, and the blind crowded into all five of them. Jesus asked the man if he wanted to be healed, and the man explained why he had not had any chance of cure all those years. Jesus told him to forget about going into the pool. He healed him on the spot, and when he told him to pick up his pallet and walk, the healed man found immediately that he had the strength to do so.

Some exegetes, ancient and modern, believe there may be an underlying symbolism in this account. They think the five porches around the pool represent the five books of the Law, that the thirty-eight years the man has been coming to the pool stand for the thirty-eight years the children of Israel were in the wilderness before they essayed to fight their way into the promised land (Deut. 2:14). Be that as it may, the crippled man found nothing in his religious tradition to cure him until Jesus came along and restored strength and action to his impotent limbs.

Earlier in the Gospel, John used water as the sign of cleansing (baptism) and as the sign of new life (a well of water within a person producing everlasting life). Now he uses it as a sign of healing. But not in itself alone. It takes the power of Jesus to make water an effective spiritual instrument. Indeed, this miracle teaches, water can be dispensed with altogether when the living source of all spiritual power, Jesus Christ, is at hand.

Rites and ritual, ceremonies and public services of worship are only means to an end. Even the church itself is but instrumental. Jesus Christ is the end of every means, the reason the church exists. Everything else in the Christian religion is auxiliary to him and finds its purpose in helping all persons to come to him and to give themselves to him, proclaiming him Savior and God.

The lame man, now cured, was apprehended by the Jewish authorities for carrying his pallet on the sabbath. He explained to them that he had been lame and, therefore, lying on it until a short while ago. This was the only way he had of getting it home. And the man who had healed him told him it was all right to take up his pallet and walk away with it. If that man had power enough to heal him, which they obviously did not have, then his authority, at least to him, superseded theirs. So he would proceed with his pallet home. Afterwards Jesus identified himself to the man and told him not to sin any more lest a worse tragedy befall him.

Wholeness is not just physical. There is a spiritual dimension to it. One is not really well unless his or her soul is well and at peace with God. "You may think you had it tough when you were lame," Jesus' remark implies, "but you have not begun to experience trouble until you let sin take possession of your soul. Then you will wish you were lame again."

The healed invalid identified Jesus to his Jewish critics. Why? We do not know. Maybe to take the "heat" off himself. Is this an instance of plea bargaining in the New Testament? "I will tell you who violated the sabbath by curing me if you won't prosecute me for doing the same by carrying my pallet." Or maybe it was to point out in pride his discovery of one whose power was greater than that of the angel who stirred the waters in Bethesda pool and gave to them the property of healing. The Jewish authorities accosted

Jesus and demanded of him an explanation for violating the sabbath.

Note the difference in the Johannine explanation from the explanation given in the synoptics. Mark says simply: "The sabbath was made for man, not man for the sabbath; so the Son of man is lord even of the sabbath" (Mark 2:27–28, RSV). Matthew contends that if the priests in the Temple are permitted to work by offering their sacrifices on the sabbath, then certainly he who is "greater than the temple" can do his work on the sabbath as well (Matt. 12:6). Luke affirms that if an ox can be pulled out of the ditch on the sabbath, then without question a human being ought to be healed on that day (Luke 13:15–17; 14:5–6). Mark's argument is utilitarian, Matthew's equalitarian, and Luke's humanitarian. But John gives a theological argument. "If my Father works on the sabbath," John quotes Jesus as saying, "then I can work, too" (5:17, AP).

When a son disobeyed his father and asserted his own will in contradiction to his parent's, the rabbis interpreted his action to imply that the son thought he was equal in every way to his father. So in this instance, the Jewish authorities understood Jesus to mean that he put himself above the Law, above revelation, above the prophets and seers of the Old Testament. They thought he equated his action with the action of God and assumed an equality with God. Therefore, they determined "to kill him" (5:18).

The Jewish leaders had correctly assessed Jesus' attitude toward himself in relationship to God the Father. He did believe that he was God's only begotten son. But they were entirely wrong in the reason they gave for his conviction that he was equal with God. It did not spring out of disobedience to his heavenly Father or his feeling that equality meant independence. Rather, its ground was that of mutual sharing, a son so in harmony with his father, so alike in purpose, disposition, and will that father and son would be incapable of disagreeing with one another. Jesus testified that everything he does happens because of his Father, whose actions he imitates. God heals diseases and corrects deformities. That is why Jesus cured the lame man at the Pool of Bethesda.

But he will do far more than this. Because God raises the dead and gives life to the lifeless, the son of God will do the same. The Father gives the right of judgment to his son. Therefore, it behooves everyone to accept the son and honor him as one would the Father if a person expects to escape judgment and receive eternal life. When the son speaks, those who are in the tombs will hear his voice and come forth. If they are good, they will receive life; if they are evil, judgment and punishment. Jesus can do nothing of himself. He utters the speech and judgment of the Father who sent him.

John the Baptist testified to the validity of Jesus' mission. But the works Jesus did testified even more convincingly to the same. There is no point in the Jews' trying to set Moses in opposition to him, Jesus said, for it was he of whom Moses prophesied. Indeed, all the scriptures point directly to him. God himself witnesses to him through the very fact that he sent him. Therefore, the healing of the lame man is a divine deed.

The Feeding of the Five Thousand and Its Meaning (6:1–71)

This miracle is recorded in all four Gospels. John, since he wrote his Gospel last, was probably familiar with the contents of the other three. When he uses common material with them, he usually follows the pattern and arrangement of Luke. But in this instance, he takes the presentations of Matthew and Mark and places the walking on the water in the storm immediately after the feeding of the five thousand. His transition and emphasis are his own and clearly indicate that he intends all the material in chapter 6 to be related to this one incident, so that the two miracles and the teachings they inspire constitute a single gospel lesson. That lesson is the sufficiency of Jesus for everything.

John adds two preliminary details that the synoptics overlook. One is that the miracle took place in the hills on the eastern shore of the Sea of Galilee. The other is that the time was the season of Passover. This second detail helps us establish the fact that Jesus' earthly ministry was at least three years in duration. He observed three Passovers after his baptism by John the Baptist. John's purpose in adding these details is neither geographical nor historical but altogether theological. Hills are suggestive of prophecy and instruction, as in the case of the Sermon on the Mount in Matthew. And the Passover is the feast of sacrifice and atonement, when the high priest from the Holy of Holies sends the lamb carrying the sins of the people to its death.

In recounting the miracle itself, John has Jesus notice the approaching crowd and say to Philip before the crowd even arrives, "How are we to buy food for so many?"

"We can't," Philip replied. "It will take two hundred pennies, or denarii, to feed that many." A denarius was a day's pay for an unskilled worker in Jesus' day. It would have taken the wages of two hundred days of labor to feed that crowd. Only a very rich person could have satisfied their hunger.

Nonetheless, the lunch of a poor boy did it. Andrew had more discernment than Philip. At least he pointed out the fact that one boy had five barley loaves and two fish. But his faith stopped there. He gave up. "But what's that," he said, "among so many people?" It was more than enough. Those who wanted had more than one helping of food. Five thousand people were fed, and there were twelve baskets of food left over. The amount of food the boy brought for his lunch was unimportant. The fact that he contributed it to Jesus made all the difference. The use Jesus put it to satisfied the hunger of a multitude.

Our weakness is strength in the hands of God. And Jesus makes our poverty rich. John is the only evangelist that tells us the bread was made of barley meal. That is how we know the boy was poor. Barley was fed to animals by the prosperous, but the poor used it to make their bread.

The feeding of the multitude got an immediate response. The people were so impressed that they attempted to crown Jesus their king. According to John, the Galileans were the first to express openly their recognition of Jesus as the Messiah. They did not wait until Jesus' triumphal entry into Jerusalem. They were correct in realizing that their true destiny lay with Jesus. He alone possessed the means that would enable them to fulfill it. In truth, he was their Messiah. But they were entirely wrong in what they took their destiny to be. It was not that they should possess an earthly kingdom with their own Jewish king. Jesus' conception of Messiah was not the same as theirs. So Jesus withdrew from them.

The disciples started back to Capernaum in a boat at night, a trip that is always risky on the Sea of Galilee. This body of water is calm one moment and wild and unruly the next. Climatic conditions change quickly on that small body of water, where calm readily and unpredictably gives place to storm. When the disciples had traveled three or four miles, high winds developed. The sea began to rise up in waves and to toss their boat up and down. Then it was that they saw Jesus walking out to them. And they were more frightened by the sight of someone walking on the water than they were of the angry sea itself. This is the only incident that John records of the disciples being afraid of their own master.

Did they think Jesus was a ghost? Or did they recognize him to be someone so akin to God that it was dangerous for them to be close to him? According to the Old Testament, for one to see God means for that person instant death. Indeed, the primary attitude one must take to God is the attitude of fear. "The fear of the Lord is the beginning of wisdom" (Psalm 111:10). But Jesus reassured them by saying: "It is I; be not afraid" (6:20). From this experience, the disciples realized the all-sufficiency of their master. He did not need the five loaves and two fish of the boy to feed the multitude. He could create out of nothing as God himself creates. And they had no need to fear him, although he possessed all the power of God, because his intention always was to use his power in their behalf.

The people whom Jesus had fed took boats the next day and went back to Capernaum. They found him there with his disciples. But they had seen the disciples leave without him, and they observed only one boat at the dock, so they said to Jesus, "How did you get here?" Jesus ignored their questions and abruptly accused them of seeking him for the material satisfaction he might give and disregarding the true nature of the miracles he had performed for them. These were the people who had tried to crown him king and who wanted from him a prosperous, powerful, secure, and independent nation in which to live. All these things would perish, Jesus told them. They worked hard to earn a living, to provide well for themselves and their families. But it was far more important for them to seek "everlasting life," which only he can give them. They expressed their willingness to do the work of God if he would tell them what that work is and would confirm the validity of what he says by performing a miracle comparable to the miracle Moses performed when he gave their ancestors manna in the wilderness. Jesus responded by saying that Moses had not given them manna. It was God himself who provided them with it out of heaven.

And now, Jesus told them, the bread God wants to give them is one who is come down out of heaven in order to give life to the world. When they cried out, "Lord, evermore give us this bread" (6:34), Jesus identified himself to them as that bread. He assured them that whoever accepts him shall never hunger or thirst again. The real lesson of the feeding of the five thousand was not that their physical hunger had been satisfied but rather that he who fed them was himself the source of their spiritual well-being and the means of their receiving everylasting life. It is the intention of the Father, Jesus assured them, to give all of these to his son, so that the son might confer on them everlasting life.

The miracle of the feeding on the hills above the lake was only to whet the appetite of the multitude for the food of God which is imperishable and supplies strength to live with God forever. That food is Jesus Christ himself.

This truth comes to view in the debate between Jesus and the Jews, who criticized him for claiming to have come down from heaven. They knew his father and mother from Nazareth. Perhaps the older among them remembered the time of the census and the very day he was born in Bethlehem. At least, they recalled vividly when he came back to Nazareth with his parents out of Egypt. How ridiculous it is for him to say that he came directly from God out of heaven! Maybe they misunderstood him. No, they did not. They had heard him correctly. But they could not appreciate what they heard.

Their ancestors had eaten the divine manna in the wilderness, yet all of them had died. They would die, too. Only those could come to Jesus whom the Father sent to him. Obviously these critics, due to their own recalcitrance, would never be sent. Jesus affirms that he is the living bread whom if a person eats thereof will never die. The bread that he gives is his own flesh. He gives it freely for the salvation of the world. In Jesus, both the gift and the giver are one and the same. Salvation is not a mere property or impersonal bequest from God to us. It is the Savior himself.

This truth caused a dispute among his Jewish critics. How could persons by eating the flesh of a man thereby derive everlasting life? Some thought this was cannibalism. Others perhaps tried to spiritualize it and give it some rational meaning. Jesus did not relieve their dispute but rather interrupted it by adding that they had to drink his blood as well. To ingest blood in any way was a sacrilege to the Jews. Meat had to be strained of any blood for a Jew to eat it. But Jesus said only as people eat his flesh and drink his blood can he dwell in them and they in him. As he lives by the Father, so they must live by him.

With that assertion, many of his followers left him as well. He said in explanation, "I am speaking to you about spirit. Spirit quickeneth. Flesh profiteth nothing" (6:63 AP). "If you are shocked now by what I say, what will your reaction be when you see me ascend up to where I was before?" (6:62, AP). What he meant was that they must desire him so much and he must become so much a part of them that they will digest him and his spirit as they would food in their bodies. As a person cannot live without food, neither can a person live without him.

When he saw so many of his followers leave him, he asked his disciples if they would do the same. It was Peter who spoke for all of them. "Lord, to whom shall we go? thou has the words of eternal life" (6:68). Yet even one of them, Jesus admitted, was a devil.

There is no guarantee of salvation even to a disciple.

Anyone, no matter what his or her spiritual state may be, can desert the Savior. The crowd that ate the loaves and fish and were so satisfied by what Jesus did for them in the hills above the sea that they wanted to crown him king left when he explained to them what life with him was really like. Even so, those whom God will send to him as his very own must want to come, must remain with him and adopt his ways, if they are to be the recipients from him of everylasting life.

Back Again in Jerusalem (7:1–53)

John compresses into a single verse what the synoptics devote most of their narratives in describing, that is, Jesus' Galilean ministry. It is the verse that opens chapter 7. The healing of the lame man had taken place in Jerusalem. The feeding of the five thousand was in Galilee. Jesus subsequently returned again to Jerusalem to the Feast of Tabernacles.

Though this feast was less important than Passover, it was nevertheless more popular. It was like Christmas is to us in comparison with Easter. Christmas is the most popular day in the Christian year. The Feast of Tabernacles came at the best season of the year, in autumn, at harvest time. It lasted eight days. The weather was generally warm but invigorating. The pilgrims lived outdoors and pitched tents in all the open spaces of the city and in the surrounding countryside. Water was brought from the Pool of Siloam to fill a golden bowl in the courtyard of the Temple for libations. Candles in golden candlesticks brightened the courtyard of the Gentiles, and every home in the city copied the practice with candles of its own in its courtyard. The people, as at Mardi Gras, had a good time.

The brothers of Jesus, presumably older than he and by a previous marriage of Joseph, probably had been embarrassed by his reception in Galilee. Like those followers who doubted, they could not convince themselves that he was the Messiah. They did not believe in him, although they wanted to believe. They, therefore, counseled him to go to Jerusalem and do his mighty works there, where all the prophets had spoken and where there would be an attentive crowd. Perhaps there he would be able to win the public. At least, he should leave

Galilee, they said. That would relieve their embarrassment over him as well as give him a fresh start—a new chance.

Jesus disregarded their advice. He did leave Galilee, but only after they had gone and the other pilgrim bands had made their way to the holy city. So he went on his own. He came late to the Feast of Tabernacles. Indeed, he evidently wanted people to miss him. In his absence, people evaluated him and his works. Some thought he was a mountebank and a fake. But others who appreciated his deeds insisted he was "a good man" (7:12). "Good" meant more to them than it does to us. Only God is good. To call Jesus "good" was to admit he was like God.

Jesus came secretly to Jerusalem. He entered the city incognito. He deliberately created disappointment in the crowds over his absence. He made them think he would not come. By waiting until the middle of the feast days to disclose himself, he intensified the excitement of the people over receiving him when he did reveal his presence to them.

Suddenly, the Lord appeared in his own Temple. Jesus did not speak like just a human being. He spoke like God. How could one be so knowledgeable and have such wisdom when he had not been to a rabbinical school? The rabbis impressed the people by quoting authorities and basing their arguments on precedent. Jesus quoted no authorities but made his observations on his own. What he said was more convincing than the teaching of the rabbis. But what right had he to such authority? His right, he said, was that he had been taught. His teacher was God himself. He was not there to build up his own reputation.

Moses had given his people the Law. But Moses got that Law from God. The people believed this because they would circumcise a child on the eighth day after its birth, even if that day was the sabbath. But Jesus got his words from the same source as Moses. Yet the people accused him of sacrilege when he healed the lame man at the Pool of Bethesda on the sabbath. Isn't it more important to make a person whole that it is to circumcise a male child? "Don't be foolish," he told the people, "use good judgment. It takes good judgment to understand and to apply the Law."

But the people did not use good judgment. Rather than permit themselves to be convinced by the force of his words, which they admitted were in quality and in truth those of the Messiah, they allowed themselves to be distracted by where he came from. "Is the Christ," they said, "to come out of Galilee? The scriptures teach that the Christ is to be descended from David and to come out of Bethlehem" (7:40–41, AP). But, then, the authorities were doing nothing to stop Jesus. "Maybe," the people thought, "that they know something that we do not know. Maybe they realize he is the Messiah" (7:26, AP). "Certainly this is the man everybody knows they want to kill" (7:25, AP). "But they are afraid to do so!" they probably said.

The true Messiah, in their minds, would come from God, and, therefore, no one could know his earthly origin. But this man and his family are known of many (7:27). Here John implies, without explicitly stating, the birth of Jesus by the Virgin Mary. Jesus was not a Galilean. He had been born in David's city of Bethlehem, and his conception was divine.

On the last day of the Feast of the Tabernacles, Jesus made his supreme pronouncement. He defied the efforts of the Pharisees and Sadducees to arrest him, openly mocking them by saying he would go where they could not come (7:33–34). They thought he meant he would leave the province and teach the Greeks in other parts of the empire. The officers they sent to arrest him refused to obey their orders, giving as their reason, "No man ever spoke like this man" (7:46, RSV). Nicodemus himself disclosed his own respect for Jesus by chiding his colleagues in the Sanhedrin for being willing to condemn this man on hearsay without giving him a hearing. They taunted Nicodemus by saying, "You must be from Galilee, too. If you knew the scripture, you would realize that no prophet can come from there" (7:52, AP).

Nonetheless, despite their maneuvers, Jesus went about his work undeterred. Looking at the almost empty bowl of water from the Spring of Siloam in the court of the Temple and pointing first at it and then at himself, he said, "If you will but believe in me, out of your own heart will flow rivers of living water" (7:38, AP). Beseechingly he said, "If any one thirst, let him come to me and drink" (7:37, RSV).

The Test Case (8:1–11)

On the very next day, the day after the Feast of the Tabernacles, as Jesus was teaching the people in the courtyard of the Temple, the scribes and Pharisees brought to him a woman who had been caught in the act of committing adultery. The penalty for such a crime was death. If the woman was a virgin engaged to be married, the penalty was death by stoning. The Sanhedrin was capable of rendering such a verdict. Perhaps the woman was being carried to her judgment when Jesus was consulted.

The consultation was no more than a trick. The Pharisees knew how kind and compassionate Jesus was. If he told them to have mercy on the woman and let her go, then they could accuse him of disregarding the Law of Moses and, thereby, make him an accomplice to her crime.

Jesus dropped his head and began to scribble on the ground. Perhaps he was embarrassed by the incident and did not want to look up at the woman and further embarrass her. All he said was, "Let him that is without sin cast the first stone" (8:7, AP). With that remark, they all began to fall away, from the eldest to the youngest. The elderly were probably first. They knew by long experience how easy it is to see faults in others and overlook worse faults in one's self. The young people soon followed.

When Jesus looked up, only the woman was there. "Evidently," he said, "you don't have any accusers any more. You are free. I don't accuse you either. Go your way, and sin no more" (8:10–11, AP).

Three mighty deeds stand out in this section of the Gospel: the healing of the lame man at the Pool of Bethesda in Jerusalem, the feeding of the five thousand in Galilee, and now this act of liberation and forgiveness again in Jerusalem.

The deeds of God are not just physical. They are moral as well. This beautiful act of compassion is the noblest of the three deeds Jesus did. Jesus saved a guilty woman from death at the hands of her moralistic accusers. And at the same time, he saved her from herself. The penalty she was about to receive was self-imposed. This young woman had committed the crime and fully deserved the punishment. She had been justly sentenced according to Moses' ancient Law. But Jesus gave her a new start. He gave her the incentive to sin no more.'

CHAPTER FOUR

THE INCARNATE LIGHT

John 8:12–10:21

WILLIAM HOLMAN HUNT'S picture of Jesus, standing in the dark with a lantern in his hand, though a masterpiece of art, is hardly adequate for its caption: "The Light of the World." The lantern does not even illuminate the garden in which the Savior stands.

John's portrayal of Jesus in this short section of his Gospel as the Light of the world, and from which Hunt got his theme, is more than adequate. It is overpowering. The light Jesus sheds is not a single beam that illuminates one dark spot on which it is focused. It is the all-pervading light of God that dispels all darkness and changes night into day for them on whom it shines.

John portrays Jesus as the incarnate light of God, the glory of the Father reflected in the countenance of his own dear son.

The Divine Light in Human Focus (8:12–29)

The sun gives the light of day. When it is focused on a part of the earth, the lands on which it shines enjoy what we call "day," a period of time in which most people are awake. The part of the earth which revolves away from the sun is in darkness. The time when we are without its light we call "night." Then it is that most people sleep. They get their rest and are renewed in strength for the activities of the next day, when their part of the earth faces the sun again. The moon and the stars provide dim light at night. But their light is insufficient. Artificial illumination is necessary for most human activities at night.

The Feast of Tabernacles, though it came at harvest time, was a celebration of God's guidance of his people in the wilderness. The Jews wandered for forty years in the wilderness. They were nomads dependent upon their flocks and herds. They lived out of doors in tents. Indeed, their place of worship was a movable tabernacle. When they left one camp, they took it down only to put it back up again when they stopped at another campsite. Their daily reminder of God was the Ark of the Covenant, a movable object that the priests carried before the people on their long march out of Egypt across the wilderness toward the promised land. While they were in camp, the Ark of the Covenant rested in the Holy of Holies inside the Tabernacle.

God led his people throughout their wilderness journeys by a pillar of cloud by day and a pillar of fire by night. The pillar of fire enlightened their path and kept them from stumbling or going astray.

All these lessons from their history were enforced on the minds of the Jewish people during the eight days of the Feast of Tabernacles. They made the past vivid in their present by staying out of doors and sleeping in tents, as we do on a camping trip, during the days of the feast.

They opened the Feast of Tabernacles by lighting four golden candlesticks in the Court of the Women in the Temple at Jerusalem. The citizens of the city responded by lighting candlesticks in the courtyards of their homes. So the whole city was aglow with light during the time of the feast.

Jesus stood in the Court of the Women. Pointing to the four golden candlesticks, he said, "I am the light of the world; he who follows me will not walk in darkness, but will have the light of life" (8:12, RSV.).

We do not know whether the candles were aglow at the time he spoke or not. Probably not, since they were lit on the first night of the feast. Every indication is that Jesus gave this testimony on the last day of the feast. Whether the candlesticks were aglow or not, the force of his testimony was the same.

At any rate, what those candles represented was inadequate at best. He came to displace the dim light of tradition and ceremony with the living light of his own presence, a light that would make the night shine as the day and would give immortality to life itself.

The Pharisees protested, "You are calling attention to yourself. You are advertising your own credentials. You are glorifying yourself. Therefore, your witness cannot be true" (8:13, AP). The Pharisees based their contention on the Law. Before a report could be admitted as evidence, it had to be supported by at least two witnesses. The testimony of just one person was inadmissible as evidence. Even Jesus had admitted earlier if he bore witness to himself, his testimony would not be true (5:31). Why this contradiction?

The answer Jesus gives is that his self-testimony is God's testimony concerning him. He is but repeating to them what the Father has told him about himself. And the conditions of the Law are satisfied, too, for the Father is the other witness who testifies with the son to confirm what the son has said. "If that is true," the Pharisees contend, "produce that second witness. Where is the Father?"

"He is not where you think he is," Jesus replies. "If you knew me, knew really who I am, you would know the Father also" (8:19–20, AP). There is a radical difference between knowing a fact and understanding the meaning of that fact. The knowledge of the senses is not the same as the knowledge of faith. The Pharisees knew their own history as well as Jesus did. But they did not realize that their history pointed to him as their Messiah.

So when he said to them that he was going to a place that they could not come, they thought he meant a place that they would not want to come. They thought he was threatening suicide. They were so amazed and self-conceited that they could not conceive of anyone not desiring the station in life that they enjoyed. Jesus' words that they were from the world below while he was from above the world were so foreign to the Pharisees' own self-estimate that they did not understand him. When he said that he spoke only for the one who sent him, they could not conceive that his reference was to God. So, in despair of helping them, Jesus admitted that they would never know who he was until he had been lifted up. He meant until he had been crucified, resurrected from the dead, and taken up into heaven. Still, whether they understood or not, everything he did was to please his heavenly Father.

The Descendants of Abraham (8:30–59)

Some of the people who heard Jesus believed what he said. At least initially, this was the case. But then, when he spoke directly to them, it appears from John's account that they hesitated and then turned back. Jesus offended them when he said to them that if they pursued his thought and advanced in their understanding of his teachings that eventually they would "know the truth" and the truth would make them "free" (8:31–32). They were offended because they thought they were already free. They knew they were offspring of Abraham. As his heirs, they had never been enslaved.

Yet they were enslaved. Their land was a conquered territory of the Roman Empire. This part of their reaction to Jesus' words is commendable. Even though under the heel of the conqueror, their spirits were not broken nor their minds enslaved. In their inner being, they knew they were free.

What is not commendable was the superficiality of their freedom. They had enslaved themselves and bound their own minds. Prejudice invariably enslaves the most agile intellects. It takes the edge off the keenest minds. By their reversion to Abraham, they shut out the new disclosure of God in Jesus. True descendants of Abraham would gladly have opened their minds and hearts to Abraham's Messiah.

Yet these people rejected him. They even conspired to murder him. They hated him so much that they had already murdered him in their heart.

"Really," Jesus said to them, "you are children of the devil. Your behavior imitates his behavior, not the behavior of Abraham." (8:39, 44, AP). This indictment Jesus made of them rests on two observations. First, he saw that they rejected the truth he taught them and preferred lies to truth. The devil is the father of lies; so in this regard, they were behaving like his children. Second, the devil is a murderer.

This desire to see him dead showed them, more than anything else, to be the devil's offspring. They were slaves, therefore, not to the Romans but to the devil. "Everyone who commits sin," Jesus told them, "is a slave to sin" (8:35, RSV). Only the son can make one free. This promise of Jesus was a reference to a custom that these people knew. A son who inherits his father's property could and often did free his father's slaves.

Abraham, in contrast to them, rejoiced in Jesus and the work he was doing. When Jesus said this, the people were dumbfounded. They said, "You are not yet fifty years old, and Abraham has been dead more than two millenia, how can you have had any contact with him?" Jesus then gave direct witness to his divinity: "Before Abraham was, I am" (8:58).

The Healing of the Blind Man (9:1–41)

After Jesus left the Temple on the last day of the Feast of Tabernacles, as he was walking with his disciples in the streets of Jerusalem, they noticed a blind man. How they knew he had been blind from birth, we are not told. Yet they did, for the disciples asked Jesus whose fault it was, the parents' or the man's, that he had been born blind.

It is easy to understand why they might have inquired about the fault of the parents. Moses taught that the sins of the fathers will be visited on the children to the third and fourth generations of the unrepentant (Exod. 20:5). But it was absurd for them to have assumed that the blind man himself could have been at fault since he was born blind. Either they believed in the foreknowledge of God which enabled God to know that the life of this person would deserve such an affliction and put it on him in advance of his sins; or else they believed so intensely in original sin that they thought an unborn child could actually sin in the mother's womb and so be personally responsible for this affliction. There is nothing in Jewish tradition to assume either of these interpretations; so this attitude of the disciples is incomprehensible.

They, as we often do, simply asked a question without considering its rational implication.

Jesus' answer, in part at least, is in keeping with their

inquiry. He said to them that neither the man nor his parents were at fault for his blindness. This answer is sound and conclusive. But Jesus went on to add that he was blind in order that his blindness might be used to demonstrate God's power. That answer is, at face value, unsatisfactory. God does not abuse someone in order to use that person as a demonstration of miraculous power. Such an act would be unjust. Such a deed would compromise God's character.

Therefore, the meaning of our Lord's answer is that this man's blindness was not the result of an immoral act on the part of his parents, and certainly he did nothing before birth to deserve this affliction. His condition was an unfortunate accident of nature. God did not deliberately plan it. However, since he was the way he was, his condition would give the son of God another opportunity to express his power in an act of mercy toward this blind man.

Jesus knew his time was limited in this life. Therefore, with a sense of urgency he set about to do the work the Father sent him to do. "As long as I am in the world," he said, "I am the light of the world" (9:5, RSV). The divine light can and must penetrate human darkness. Thus without any request from the blind man himself, Jesus set out to make him see.

Jesus mixed saliva from his mouth with dust from the ground to make clay that he applied to the sockets of the man's eyes. He sent the man to the Pool of Siloam to wash the clay out. Why did he do this? In order to recapitulate God's act in creation. God made the first human by using clay to mold him. God took dust from the ground watered by mist from the earth and breathed into the earthly model the breath of life (Gen. 2:6–7). This act of restoring sight to a physically blind man was to be more than a physical act. The entire man was to be made over in the process. A beggar became able to work. A weak person became courageous. An ordinary human being became an avid believer in the son of God.

The narrative rises in psychological intensity. After the man washed his eyes, he saw. At once his physical sight was complete. He had twenty-twenty vision. But when he was accosted by the Pharisees, he did not even know where Jesus was. Asked by them what he thought about the man who healed him, his answer was that he must be a prophet.

The man's parents testified that their son had been blind since birth. Then they were asked, "Does he now see?"

They answer, "You had better address that question to him. He is able enough to take responsibility for his answers. We do not want to be involved in this."

The Pharisees interrogated the man again. They told him that he should give God the praise, not the person who healed him. This person, they contended, is a sinner, for he healed him on the sabbath day. John comments that even the Pharisees are divided among themselves on this issue. Some of them realized that a sinner could not perform such a miracle. Others, however, put the observance of the sabbath day above the welfare of the people who observe it and labeled Jesus a sinner for violating it.

It is interesting that the man's own neighbors had so associated his blindness with him that once he was able to see and no longer begged for a living, they were unable to recognize him. A few admitted it must be he. Others said it was another who looked like him.

The man responded to the Pharisees that he did not know anything about Jesus' moral character, whether he was a sinner or not. "One thing I know, that, whereas I was blind, now I see" (9:25).

"How did he do this?"

The man declared impatiently, "I have told you all this before. Why do you keep on asking me? Could it be that you want to become his disciples?"

"No, no," the Pharisees said and retreated. "You only are his disciple. We are Moses' disciples. We don't even know where this man came from."

"Well, if you are as smart as you claim to be," the man replied, "you ought to know, for he healed me. He is an extraordinary person. Have you ever heard of anyone, since the world began, making a blind man see? God does not hear sinners. God hears only those who sincerely worship him. Look what God enabled this man to do for me. What he did testifies he is of God."

The Pharisees were theologically defeated by an ignorant beggar. They had no more to say. Their last words were, "Who are you, born in sin, to try to teach us?" And they ordered him out of their presence.

But Jesus found him and asked him if he now believes in the son of God. The man humbly replied, "Who is he? I want so much to believe in him."

Jesus said, "Since you now see, the person you are looking at is he." And the man believed with his whole heart and worshiped Jesus.

This blind man, because Jesus is the light of the world, both saw and perceived. But others, like the Pharisees, see but never understand the truth of what they see. They would be better off blind, for then they would not be able to see how to sin. But, as it is, they are sinners and do not know it. Jesus was a Savior to the blind man who accepted his mercy and believed in him, but he was a judge who condemned the unbelieving Pharisees.

There is a winsome and inspiring beauty about the faith of the blind man as it unfolds and intensifies in this narrative. The gift of sight was unsolicited by him. He passively accepted what Jesus bestowed. All he did was wash out his eyes. Yet his new condition enabled him to work, which he gladly did. He gave up the degrading necessity of begging. His faith expressed itself initially in self-respect. But there is the element of gratitude as well. The man who gave him his sight must be a prophet. On the basis of what Jesus had done for him, the healed person formed his estimate of Jesus. Although his parents were afraid of being ostracized simply because their son had been healed, he was willing to endure criticism and mistreatment and even expulsion from the synagogue rather than disparage Jesus. The climax of his experience was his confession that the person who healed him is the son of God. This man's faith began by loving Jesus for what Jesus had done for him. It ended by loving Jesus unselfishly for Jesus' own sake and thereby loving himself because Jesus loved him. His faith rose from a concept of God as an instrument of his own self-betterment to a concept of himself as a tool in God's hands to be used as God sees fit.

The Good Shepherd (10:1–21)

There is no transition, or abrupt departure, from the healing of the blind man and the picture of the good shepherd. Both are essential parts of the same piece, for what Jesus says about the good shepherd is occasioned by the reaction of the people to the healing and is an explanation, not of the miracle itself, but of its effects on the lives of its witnesses. Though what Jesus now says paints a picture in words, it is not a parable or even a story. It is an analogy, a simple comparison of any good shepherd to Jesus. The difference between Jesus and any ordinary shepherd is that our Lord's sheep are human beings.

The immediate meaning of what he said was apparent to his auditors. The Pharisees had not healed the blind man. They had even objected to his being healed. To them he was a nameless beggar. Jesus had healed him. He cared enough for him to come back to him again and to offer him salvation. He came to know him and to look after him as any good shepherd knows and cares for one of his sheep.

But the deeper meaning of this analogy was not apparent to any one. It was an enigma. They all were familiar with a sheepfold—an enclosed area in which many different shepherds placed their sheep and hired a gatekeeper to attend it. The gatekeeper admitted only one of the shepherds, never a stranger. The shepherds had to know their own sheep to distinguish them from the sheep of others who shared the sheepfold with them. They had to collect their sheep and take them out to pasture.

At times, sheep owners employed shepherds who did not own sheep to tend their flocks. However, one could not expect such a hired person to take the same interest in the sheep as the owner. These hirelings were interested in collecting their wages, not in the welfare of the sheep. Then in times of danger, they put their own safety above the safety of the sheep. But the shepherd who owned his sheep would take great risks to protect them. They were his property. They were his sole livelihood and the livelihood of his family.

To Jesus, the sheepfold was the safe abode of all God's people. He himself was the true shepherd who owned those sheep. Unlike any other shepherd, even those who owned sheep, he loved every one of his sheep more than he loved himself. He would go so far as to give up his life to save the life of one of his sheep. These Pharisees were no more than hirelings. They cared for their own status and self-interest above the interest of the people they were entrusted to teach. They worked only for wages—the esteem and praise of the public. They had shown no interest in the blind man whatever. But Jesus also had human sheep in other sheepfolds. He was as much interested in saving people outside the Jewish religion as he was those inside Israel. Finally, he would gather all those sheep who would follow him into the everlasting sheepfold of God.

It is no wonder many of those who heard him said he was out of his mind to talk like that. His words were still an enigma to them. Others, though they did not grasp the full import of what he said, at least appreciated what he had done. An insane person or one with a demon inside (which the people of that day believed made a person insane) could not cause a blind person to see. These people realized Jesus was the Light of the world.

CHAPTER FIVE

THE INCARNATE LIFE

John 10:22–11:57

LIFE HAS TO be incarnate. Unlike *word,* which can be written as well as spoken, or *deed,* which is always separate and distinct from the person who performs it, or even *light,* which can be distinguished from the object which generates it, *life* is inseparable from the organism which it animates and to which it gives movement and responsiveness to the environment. A living organism is entirely different from an inanimate object. But apart from the organism itself and its behavior, it is impossible to identify life as a material, or substance, that can be added to or subtracted from the organism.

All we can observe is that the organism is entirely different when it loses its life. It decays and wastes away, and we are not aware of it any more. Yet we never see or feel that life that originally gave it its nature. Life has to be in a tangible entity in order for us to be aware of it, for to us it has no being in itself. The human body is a composition of chemical elements that we find elsewhere in nature. What makes it human is its living intelligence, that is, the force of intelligent life that is incarnate within it. "And the Lord God formed man of the dust of the ground, and breathed into his nostrils the breath of life; and man became a living soul" (Gen. 2:7).

Though life is always incarnate, the degree of its intensity varies. A person is more alive than an animal, and the movement and adaptability of most animals is greater than that of fish and insects. Eternal life inheres only in the being of God, so that life in any form is God's gift. Apart from

God, there is nothing in the world that has always been alive; and everything that is alive sooner or later dies. For a person to have his or her life restored to that person after death, the restoration can come only from the hands of God.

Therefore, the incarnate life that John presents is divine and eternal life, not its human derivative, and this life finds tangible expression in the person of Jesus Christ and him alone. He is the personification of God's own everlasting life. And it is a person's attachment to him and belief in him that guarantees that person eternal life. "Jesus said unto her, I am the resurrection, and the life: he that believeth in me, though he were dead, yet shall he live" (John 11:25).

The Feast of Dedication (10:22–42)

What we dealt with in the last chapter took place before, during, and just after the Feast of Tabernacles, an appropriate season for Jesus to declare himself to be the Light of the world. What we are to discuss now begins three months after that feast. Fall has given way to winter. The harvests of autumn have been displaced by the rains and cold when everything has been stored into barns and the fields await a later time for sowing.

The Feast of the Dedication of the Temple came in December; it was based on an important event in Jewish history. Antiochus Epiphanes, who ruled the Asiatic segment of the Greek empire, had set up an idol in the Temple in Jerusalem. This act desecrated it, making it unsuitable to the Jews as a place of worship. What he did was known as "the abomination of desolation." In 165 B.C., Judas Maccabaeus, after a successful revolt against the Greek overlord, cleansed the Temple and made it a fit place for worship again. The Feast of Dedication celebrated this event. It was not one of the great biblical feasts which recalled watershed events in the Old Testament. Its origin was later, going no further back than the intertestamentary period. It did not compare in importance or length of celebration with the Passover or the Feast of Tabernacles, for that matter. But it was a feast. And it was on the calendar of any pious Jew who had the leisure to observe it. Jesus was on hand in Jerusalem to keep it. Indeed, John implies that our Lord never left Jerusalem between Tabernacles and Dedication. Evidently he did not go anywhere between the two feasts.

Although the obvious reference of Dedication was the cleansing of the Temple by Judas Maccabaeus, it had at this time a covert meaning which to the Jewish mind was more poignant. The Maccabean period was the last epoch of Jewish independence. It was the period of freedom just before the Roman conquest. As a result, the Jews celebrated it more intensely than they would otherwise. It reminded them of God's promise of a Messiah, a deliverer, who would restore them to their former power and glory, giving them their freedom.

Therefore, John's chronological reference to the date when the Jews asked Jesus what to both them and him was the supreme question is a theological reference as well. As the earlier Feast of Tabernacles symbolized the incarnation, God's tabernacle with his people in the person of his own son, so this later Feast of Dedication symbolized the dedication of the son of God to his mission, the climax of which would be his voluntary sacrifice of himself for the sins of humanity.

On this feast, the Jews asked Jesus not to keep them in suspense any longer but to tell them frankly whether he was their Messiah or not. Jesus responded that he has been trying to tell them ever since he began his mission but that they have been too stubborn to believe him. He pointed to the works he had done among them. These works were testimony aplenty to who he was. He said that they have been unable to believe because they don't really belong to him. Only those who had had the hardihood to follow him were really his. What God had given, no one could allure away. Jesus' followers were his always to keep. Then came the supreme declaration. This is the Gospel's clap of thunder. Jesus declared: "I and my Father are one" (10:30).

The Jews went wild at the utterance of these words. To equate one's self with God was blasphemy to them. They picked up stones to kill Jesus on the spot. Before they could hurl them, however, he mocked them by asking, "For what good work now will you kill me?"

"Good work!" they retort. "Do you consider blasphemy good? How can you, a mere man, make yourself God?"

"Why your own Law," Jesus claims, "supports my contention. It describes as gods those to whom the work of God was given." At this point, Jesus quoted from the Book of Psalms, where it is written: "I have said, Ye are gods; and all of you are children of the Most High" (Psalm 82:6). "If this can be said of mere mortals like yourselves, why is it blasphemy for him whom the Father consecrated and sent to refer to himself as the Son of God?" (10:35–36, AP).

The test is the quality of the work. "If you can't believe in my own personal authenticity, then evaluate if what I do is what God himself would do if he were in my place; then accept the value and authenticity of my works. If you do, you will then realize that the Father is in me and that I am in the Father" (10:37–38, AP).

Indeed, the very life of God is incarnate in his son.

At this point, since the leaders of Jewry were out to kill him, Jesus left Jerusalem and repaired beyond Jordan to the place where his public ministry began. He went to the very site where John the Baptist baptized and where he himself had been heralded as the lamb of god who takes away the sins of the world. To be sure, John the Baptist was no longer there. He was dead, but the memory of his testimony to Jesus lived on. The people admitted that the Baptist performed no miracles, but everything he had said about Jesus proved to be true. Many now believed Jesus to be the son of God.

Those who did believe came out to him in the wilderness just as folk had gone out to John the Baptist before him. True belief initiates action on the part of the believer. Once people are convinced, they bestir themselves and move on their own initiative toward God.

It is important to realize that Jesus went to the site where the Israelites under Joshua made their entrance into the promised land. Jesus was ready to make his entrance as well. He would recapitulate the history of his people. But his conquest would be different from theirs. They won geographical territory for themselves in order to build a nation. Jesus would give himself up in order to build the kingdom of God in the hearts of all believers. He would enter the promised land in order to bring the life of God which he uniquely possessed to those who will receive it.

The Raising of Lazarus from the Dead (11:1–44)

John records only six miracles Jesus performed. Five of these are unique to his Gospel. Only in the miracle of the feeding of the five thousand does he report one of the miracles which the synoptics relate. The raising of the dead by Jesus is not peculiar to the Fourth Gospel, however. Mark tells that he raised the daughter of Jairus from the dead (Mark 5:21–43). And Luke reports the restoration of life which Jesus gave to the widow's son as he was being carried out in a funeral procession through the gate of the city of Nain to the cemetery (Luke 7:11–17). Even so, the raising of Lazarus is different from the other two. They appear as further and more impressive examples of our Lord's miraculous power and therefore take their place alongside his other mighty acts. But the raising of Lazarus is much more than an example of Jesus' gifts as a worker of miracles. It is God's display of himself in and through Jesus as the source of life and its preserver beyond time and throughout all eternity. This is John's proof that the Father was with and in his son, the evidence of Jesus' affirmation: ''I and my Father are one'' (10:30).

This miracle is the climax of the Fourth Gospel. Jesus, in bringing himself to Lazarus, brought him new life as well. Jesus performed this his last and greatest miracle on the eve of his own passion. Soon he would be doomed to death. The life he gave another was presented under the shadow of his own death. Nonetheless, what our Lord did in raising Lazarus from the dead is the supreme demonstration that he is God's life incarnate and that the life he brings is not diminished by death. ''Verily, verily, I say unto you, The hour is coming, and now is, when the dead shall hear the voice of the Son of God: and they that hear shall live'' (5:25).

Jesus was still on the other side of the Jordan River

when he received word that Lazarus was ill. The evangelist does not tell us the nature of that illness or how grave it was, but we presume it was serious, else Jesus would not have been informed of it at all. The context implies that with the message comes also the urgent request that Jesus come and cope with it. The evangelist does tell us that the sick man, Lazarus, and his two sisters were very close friends of Jesus.

Jesus responded, "This illness is not unto death; it is for the glory of God, so that the Son of God may be glorified by means of it" (11:4, RSV). Yet, in the light of what follows, Jesus could not mean by this that Lazarus would not die. The disciples took him to mean that. They were more fearful of Jesus' safety if he returned to Jerusalem than they were of Lazarus' demise. Their response was that he will recover anyway. Why should Jesus bother to go to him? Why should he take any risks with his own life? Jesus had said to them, "Lazarus is asleep, and I must wake him" (11:11, AP). If he is just asleep, they retorted, he will eventually wake up of his own accord. Jesus had to be candid with them and tell them outright that Lazarus was dead.

There are other instances in the New Testament when "fall asleep" is used as a synonym for death (Acts 13:36; 1 Cor. 11:30; 15:16–20; 1 Thess. 4:13). As a result of Jesus' usage of sleep in relationship to death, this wording is familiar among peoples where Christianity is prevalent.

Light and life are affixed to one another in this incident. When the disciples remonstrated with Jesus, warning him of the danger he faced in returning to Jerusalem, he said that there are only twelve hours in a day. One walking in daylight will not stumble, because the light of the world is evident. One walking at night is apt to stumble, because the light is gone. Literally speaking, this observation of Jesus is out of context and has no relevance to the issue under discussion. But symbolically understood, it means that Jesus carries light with him, for he is the Light of the world, and that light gives the power of life to any who believe.

Jesus deliberately tarried two days after he received the message. He told the disciples that he was glad he was not in Bethany when Lazarus was taken ill. Otherwise, he would have healed him as he had healed others. Now he will perform a far greater miracle, which would confirm their belief and strengthen their witnessing.

Thomas, who later would doubt that it was Jesus who was raised from the dead, at this point insisted that he and the others accompany Jesus so that if he should be killed they would be killed with him.

Lazarus had expired before Jesus ever got the message of his illness. The evangelist tells us that when Jesus did arrive in Bethany, Lazarus had been buried four days.

Bethany is in easy walking distance of Jerusalem, only two miles away on the other side of the Mount of Olives. Bethany lies on the eastern slope facing Jericho and the Dead Sea. Jesus had come from the other side of the River Jordan, crossing the wilderness of Judea en route. Indeed, he must have been some place almost midway between Jerusalem and Mount Nebo, from the peak of which Moses had seen the promised land. Consequently he had a long, hard journey on foot to Bethany.

Jewish friends had come from nearby Jerusalem to comfort Lazarus's two sisters, Martha and Mary, in their grief. Then news arrived that Jesus, too, was on his way to lend them the strength of his presence in this time of deep sorrow. When Martha heard that he was approaching the village, she ran out to meet him. Mary was too disconsolate to leave the house. She was more introverted than Martha; her thoughts were turned inward.

When Martha encountered Jesus, she greeted him with the desperate, agonizing exclamation: "Lord, if only you had been here, my brother would not have died!" (11:21, AP) Then she added, wistfully, longingly, not quite daring to hope, "But I know, that even now, whatsoever thou wilt ask of God, God will give it thee" (11:22).

Jesus' response, though positive, was not positive enough for her. When our Lord said, "Thy brother shall rise again," Martha replied, "O, I know that. We all shall rise again on the last day." Then our Lord made the cataclysmic announcement that he himself is the incarnate life of God that can never die and that he is capable of bestowing that life on any who also will receive it. "He that believeth in me, though he were dead, yet shall he live: and whosoever liveth and believeth in me shall never die" (11:25–26).

"Martha," he said calmly, "do you believe this?"

"Yes, Lord," she replied, "for I realize you are the son of God." What Martha longed for but really dared not hope would happen, she sensed now was about to take place. She was standing in the presence of God's eternal life personified in the human Jesus.

Evidently Jesus asked where Mary was. No doubt, he was disappointed that she had not come out with her sister to greet him, for Martha went swiftly to her, saying, "The Master is come, and calleth for thee" (11:28). John tells us she spoke to Mary secretly. Why? We do not know. Perhaps she wanted Mary to see him alone. But, if this was her reason, she was thwarted; because the Jewish mourners, thinking Mary was going to the tomb to weep there for her brother, followed her. They were all about her when she reached Jesus. Her greeting was precisely the same as her sister's had been: "If only you had been here, my brother would not have died" (11:32, AP).

But Jesus' response was entirely different. When he saw her and her entourage both weeping, he groaned and was troubled. The Greek language conveys the implication that he was disgusted. Disgusted at the Jews because they were professional mourners. They did what they did for a fee. And troubled with Mary that she had become disconsolate to the point of being hysterical. She lost control of herself because of her grief. But when they took Jesus to Lazarus' burial place, he wept, too. His weeping was noticeable, for the Jews said, "See how he must have loved him!" (11:36, AP).

But others, more skeptical, said, "Couldn't this man who opened the eyes of the blind have kept Lazarus from dying?"

All admitted what Jesus might have done while Lazarus was still alive. None even began to imagine what Jesus could do and would do now that Lazarus was dead.

Suddenly the action changed. Jesus did not respond to what he found in this mournful situation. He created an entirely different situation. He seized the initiative. He did not respond just in comforting and understanding love to the death of a friend, trying to bring solace and peace to his disturbed family. No, immediately he dispelled sorrow with joy and transformed tragedy into triumph. He commanded that the stone at the mouth of the tomb be rolled aside, even though Martha protested that her brother's body would already have begun to decay and the odor from it would be unbearable.

Nonetheless, Jesus cried out, "Lazarus, come forth!" And he who was dead stood before them alive, still bound, hand and foot, in his grave clothes. "Loose him," Jesus said, "and let him go" (11:44).

The miracle of miracles had taken place. Death had been displaced by life through the power of the incarnate life of God.

Reaction and Interpretation (11:45–57)

Seeing is believing. The Jewish mourners could not possibly deny what they had witnessed. A man they had helped to bury, whose death they had mourned, one who had been in the tomb four days, was now as much alive as they were. There was no way they could dispute such evidence.

Perhaps all present accepted the evidence, but some did not subscribe to the teaching of him who supplied that evidence. They could accept the fact that Jesus raised Lazarus from the dead. This does not mean, however, that they had to accept Jesus as their master and Savior as well. Some did. Others did not. Those who did not reported to the Pharisees what they had seen.

Thaumaturgists (miracle workers) abounded in Jesus' day. The magicians could do amazing and incredible things. To some spectators, Jesus was just another magician, the greatest of the lot, no doubt, but not necessarily deserving of anything more than a magician's fame.

In order to disabuse the minds of his audience that he belonged to the magicians' trade, Jesus had prayed *aloud* to the Father and asked his help in restoring Lazarus from death to life. He had done this entirely for the sake of his onlookers. He did not need to do it. The will of the Father is the same as the will of the son. Jesus knew in advance that he had the full support and help of his heavenly Father. He did not need to pray for anything. But he wanted the people to know that the miracle he was about to perform was done in compliance with the will of God, so that they might correctly interpret his action as God's will.

You and I have to pray. Our wills are not always in harmony with the will of God. When we make petitions, we close our requests with the submissive acknowledgement: "Not my will but thy will be done." It was impossible for Jesus not to express in action as well as thought the will of his heavenly Father.

It is interesting that the Sanhedrin itself was convinced when the news reached Jerusalem that Jesus had raised a man from the dead. Evidently the evidence for the miracle was so strong that even this body did not question its authenticity. The concern of the Sanhedrin was that Jesus' power would win the allegiance of most of the people to him. Because of the structure of his teachings and the loyalty of the people to him, they worried that he would precipitate a revolt from Rome. This would lead to the destruction of the Temple and the massacre of the Jewish people. Therefore, the Sanhedrin began to conspire to put Jesus to death. "It is better," the high priest said, "for one man to die than to allow the whole nation to perish."

Caiaphas did not really comprehend the truth of his own advice. Jesus would die on the cross as a sacrifice for the sins of humanity and thereby, in his own oblation of himself once offered, be a full and sufficient sacrifice for all humankind. His death would spiritually enable all who believe on him to live. But, on the other hand, what Caiaphas proposed would not spare his own people. Jerusalem and its Temple would be destroyed and the Jewish people decimated. Caiaphas's advice was ironic.

The plot against Jesus led him to return for a time to the town of Ephraim on the edge of the wilderness. The populace of Jerusalem, knowing that the authorities were determined to arrest and perhaps kill Jesus, wondered whether or not he would attend the Feast of the Passover that year. He would attend, but he would bide his time. He knew he would become the sacrificial lamb, but he wanted to await the exact time for its offering.

John records only six miracles out of all that Jesus performed. But in recording these six, he spelled out his Christology. Jesus is adequate for the whole needs of humanity:

1. He satisfies all legitimate human desires by supplying wine from water at a wedding feast.
2. He cures a child about to die of what appeared to be an incurable disease.
3. He makes a lame man walk.
4. He feeds a multitude who have no bread or meat.
5. He gives sight to a blind man. Indeed, all facets of human need are met by him.
6. He calls a person from death back to life again, proving thereby that even "the dead shall hear the voice of the Son of God, and they that hear shall live" (5:25).

CHAPTER SIX

THE INCARNATE WAY

John 12:1–13:38

WHAT JESUS WAS as Word, Deed, Light, and Life makes him the perfect example for living as God intends that all people should live. Irenaeus pointed out long ago that humanity had become so corrupted by sin that no one knew how a person created in the image of God was expected to live. Jesus, therefore, as the perfect Person demonstrates the pattern of behavior for all to emulate.

The early Christians were known as followers of the way. That way was the way of salvation. In this section of his Gospel, John presents Jesus as the incarnate Way, the divine intention for life demonstrated in human form.

Indeed, there is a major division in the Fourth Gospel between the material that ends with chapter 11 and that which follows. The first part of the Gospel presents the six miracles or great signs—the mighty demonstrations of God's power and grace in the person of his own dear son.

But from chapter 12 to the end of the Gospel we see what happens as Jesus closes his public ministry and endures his passion. John represents the passion as an act of God in the drama of our redemption.

In this opening part of the second section, John presents Jesus as the incarnate Way of God that all persons should follow. As the writer does this, he describes important instances in which both individual persons and people in general take Jesus' way as their way, thereby demonstrating some aspect of salvation.

Adoration (12:1–11)

Jesus returned to Bethany only six days before the

Passover he was to observe as a faithful Jew. His crucifixion was imminent. He repaired to the home of Martha and Mary and their brother Lazarus, whom only a short time before he had raised from the dead. The two sisters prepared a sumptuous meal for this friend and benefactor. But only one of them, Martha, served the meal. The brother, as head of the house, sat and ate with his guests at the table. The disciples, and perhaps others, were present.

Shortly after the news spread that Jesus had returned to Bethany, large crowds gathered about the house. They used Jesus' coming as an excuse to satisfy their curiosity. They wanted to see a man who had been dead and was alive again. Both Lazarus and Jesus, who had raised him, were subjects of their curiosity. This popularity made the chief priests determined to kill Lazarus along with Jesus. On account of what Jesus had done for Lazarus, many Jews were becoming followers of this strange new Messiah. They had left the traditional way of Judaism for the way of Jesus.

Mary, instead of waiting on the table, rubbed the feet of Jesus with expensive ointment and dried them with her own hair. The jar of ointment weighed one pound. The ointment was pure nard. It was so sweet and the odor of it so strong that it penetrated the whole house with a pleasant and soothing scent. The cost of the ointment was the equivalent of the wages of a laborer for three hundred days, almost a year.

Therefore, Judas, the treasurer of the disciples, feigned indignation over this act of prodigality and waste. He said the ointment should have been sold and the proceeds given to the poor. But the author of the Gospel adds as an aside that Judas really wanted the money for himself. "He was a thief," who all along had kept his hand in the till.

Jesus rebuked Judas. "Do not bother Mary," he said, "let her do what she is doing in anticipation of my burial." That, I think, is a more understandable rendition of the Greek text than what we find in an English translation. It implies, "You would not object to such expense for ointment if I were a corpse." Jesus adds, "You have the poor with you always. There will be many opportunities to help them. But you won't always have me."

What Mary did was unusual and altogether out of the ordinary. The custom in that day was for either the host or a servant to wash the feet of the guests when they came in from a dusty walk. Later, if the host was rich, he anointed the head of the chief guest with oil as an act of courtesy and honor. But Mary anointed Jesus' feet, massaged them with her hands, and wiped them with her hair. For a respectable woman to use her hair as a towel was degrading and frightfully immodest.

What is the explanation of all this? Keep in mind that John, in contrast to the synoptics, is a profound theologian. Everything he describes has theological significance.

1. Mary prostrated herself, literally threw herself, in complete abandon, forsaking all self-attained dignity and honor, before her Savior and God. A towel was not good enough for him. She must use her hair to dry his feet, for her hair represented herself.
2. She anointed his feet as an expression of penitence. She felt unworthy to pour oil on his head.
3. Oil was used by her, because she recognized him already as "the resurrection and the life." He had bestowed life on her brother.

This act of hers is an indication of her adoration of Jesus. By it she worshiped him as God.

And Jesus accepted it as such and commended her for it. The worship of God takes precedence over everything else. Without worship, work is trivial and ineffective. The poor could not be properly and fully served just by feeding them at the proper time and ministering to their material needs. They must be restored to the dignity of knowing that they are children of God. This cannot happen apart from the worship and love of God on the part of those who try to help the poor. The first obligation of the Christian is his or her worship of God through adoration and praise of Jesus Christ. This is the very beginning of the way of salvation.

Homage (12:12–26)

The adoration of Jesus by Mary at Bethany, an instance of an individual prostrating herself before her Lord, is followed in the Fourth Gospel by two public events in which people in general pay homage to Jesus. One includes large crowds; the other, only a small group of special people.

The first of these is the Savior's triumphal entry into Jerusalem, the very next day after Mary had anointed Jesus's feet with ointment. John's description of this event is different from the synoptics' but does not in any way contradict theirs. John leaves out some of the details they include, but he also adds some observations of his own. It is he who specifies the palm tree as providing the branches that were spread before Jesus on the road. These had been used when Judas Maccabaeus, the cleanser of the Temple and the Jewish hero who had wrested independence for his people from the Seleucid empire, was welcomed as a conqueror into his city (1 Maccabees 13:51). He also describes the entry as fulfillment of the prophecy of Zechariah in which the king will "speak peace" and forswear war (Zech. 9:9–10). Yet John tells us that even the disciples did not discern this at the time (12:16). This means that John himself did not until long after the event was past. At the time, they all, no doubt, thought that Jesus, like the others, would restore independence to his people and rule by might as any other king. John alone of the four evangelists gives an explanation for the size and enthusiasm of the crowds. The crowds were made up, on the one hand, of those who entered the city with Jesus and who had seen him raise Lazarus from the dead in Bethany and, on the other hand, of people in Jerusalem who had heard about this miracle and wanted to see the one who had performed it. The crowds were so large that the Pharisees despaired of ever stopping them and opined "the world has gone after him" (12:19, RSV).

The people cried, "Hosanna!", which means, "Save us!" And with it, they acclaimed Jesus, in messianic overtones, as Israel's king. Thus Jesus received homage from his own people, crowds of pilgrims who had come from all over the country to observe the Passover.

But Jesus also received homage from a group of foreigners. Some Greek proselytes to Judaism came to where he was at the time in Jerusalem and accosted Philip with the request, "Sir, we would see Jesus" (12:21). Philip carried this request to Andrew, and the two men together went to Jesus with it. Why did the Greeks contact Philip? Simply because *Philip* is a Greek name, and maybe they thought he was really one of them.

Jesus' response to the request of the Greeks is amazing. John does not tell us whether he actually saw them or not. All John reports is Jesus' statement to Andrew and Philip. He said that unless a grain of wheat falls into the earth and dies, it cannot bear fruit. He continued that if one loves his life and timidly holds on to it, that person will lose it. Yet if one hates his life in this world, he will recover it in the world to come. Jesus is pleased that the Greeks have taken the initiative to seek him out. He says the Father will honor all those who honor him and seek to serve him. Presumably, the Greeks did see him after all.

Obedience (12:27–50)

At this point, the author turns aside from others and their response to Jesus and focuses on Jesus himself. Like anyone else, Jesus was troubled over what he knew he must face in the next few days. Yet, at the same time, he realized that it was for this very purpose that he had come into the world. It was only through obedience to his Father that he could glorify him. His obedient suffering would bring glory to the heavenly Father; therefore, he prayed "Father, glorify thy name" (12:28).

And God answered him by saying, "Son, in you I have glorified it, and I will glorify it yet again."

Jesus heard what God said, but the people did not. Some did have enough discernment to think that an angel had spoken, but most of the folk heard only a noise. They thought it was thunder. One's soul must be in tune with the divine in order to hear God speaking.

"I must be lifted up," Jesus said, "if I am to draw all people unto me." By this he meant he must be raised up on his cross in death in order for the people to receive the full benefit of his ministry. Even so, they wouldn't be able to receive these benefits unless they could appreciate and accept him. He is the Light. They must walk in that light while it still shone among them. Otherwise, even the cross would be enveloped in darkness. He was so disappointed at their reaction that he went away and hid himself. He had come to them, his own people, only to be rejected by them.

"When Jesus had said this, he departed and hid himself from them" (12:36, RSV). This verse marks the very end of Jesus' ministry to his own people. Jesus did not address himself publicly to them any more. He abandoned them. He left them alone.

Why? Because it was futile to make any more overtures to them. Some, even those in authority, had been convinced by him and wanted to accept him, but they dared not. They were afraid of criticism from the Pharisees. They were afraid of losing their positions of prominence among the people. Those poor souls "loved the praise of people more than the praise of God" (12:45, AP).

Brokenhearted, despondent, and grieved over his own people, Jesus said: "I have not spoken on my own but for God. Those who did believe in me really believed in God. I will not judge them in the end. It is God's word that I have spoken to them that will judge and condemn them on the last day. The word I would have given them, had they let me, is the word of eternal life."

The obedience that Jesus gave to his Father he expected the people to give to him, for he had not worked from his own authority but from the authority of God who sent him.

Humble Service (13:1–17)

The synoptic Gospels divide the ministry of Jesus geographically. They deal with his work in Galilee and then describe his last week in Jerusalem. John does not stress the geographical setting for Jesus' work, although he provides more geographical details surrounding each particular event than do the rest. He reports, as we have seen, Jesus, moving back and forth from Judea to Galilee throughout the whole of his ministry, so that where he is in terms of what he does seems of minor significance. It is the meaning of the events that is of supreme importance to the author of the Fourth Gospel.

Therefore, the description of the Last Supper in John is quite different from that in the synoptic Gospels. It does not fall on the night of Passover as it does in the other three Gospels, but comes on the night before. The symbolism of the bread as Jesus' body to be eaten and the wine as his blood to be drunk by his disciples in remembrance of his death and in anticipation of his coming is not crucial to the narrative of the Fourth Gospel as it is to that of the synoptics. Indeed, John does not mention it at all. In its place, he substitutes a beautiful act of humble service, itself symbolic as well as exemplary. Jesus washes his disciples' feet.

The symbolism lies in the fact that Jesus laid aside his garments and wrapped a towel about his loins. This was the manner of the slave in a rich Roman household as he washed the feet of guests who entered for a meal. It is still the custom in Japan and other parts of the Orient to remove one's shoes as one enters a dwelling in order not to spoil the clean, polished floors of the home with dust and dirt from the outside. Since people wore open sandals in Jesus' day, their feet needed washing on entering the house. Had not our Lord divested himself of his divine majesty when he entered the world as a poor baby to reveal God to humanity? Would he not lay aside his life for the redemption of men and women by dying for their sins on the cross? This truth is symbolized for the disciples in his laying aside his garments and assuming the manner of a slave. Crucifixion was the death penalty imposed by Rome only on her conquered subjects and slaves, never on her citizens.

Peter protested that it was not appropriate for the Master to wash the feet of his disciples and that he would not permit him to wash his. Jesus said that if he did not wash Peter's feet, Peter could not become a part of him and receive the benefits of what he had come to bring. Then Peter, impetuous and emotional as he was, requested Jesus to wash him all over, head and hands as well as feet. Jesus said that this was not necessary, since he assumed that Peter had washed before he came to supper. Only his feet needed washing.

The foot bath as such is not important. The importance lay in what was symbolized in the act of him who performed it and of them who received it. Just as the bread and wine in the synoptic accounts represented Jesus' body and blood given for their redemption, so this act of humble service also bespoke Jesus' sacrificial death on the cross for their salvation. Whether they fed on him by faith in their hearts with thanksgiving by eating the bread and drinking the wine with him at meal, or whether they gratefully permitted him to wash and dry their feet before the meal in anticipation of being cleansed by his blood on the cross, the meaning of both symbols was the same: We are saved from sin and transformed into new creatures in Christ Jesus only as we freely and gladly receive from him the benefits of his passion and death on the cross for our redemption.

But this act of our Lord in washing his disciples' feet was also exemplary. He did it as an example for them to follow. Humble service to others is expected of all the followers of Jesus Christ. In the face of human need, we must lay aside all rights and privileges, all honors and evidences of attainment and worth and perform the most menial tasks that are necessary to relieve suffering and to assure the welfare of others. God performed the task of a slave for our sakes. "Verily, verily, I say unto you, The servant is not greater than his lord; neither he that is sent greater than he that sent him" (13:16).

Defection and Love (13:18–38)

At the very time that Jesus exhorted the disciples to imitate him in the act of humble service to others, he sadly admitted that his words are not applicable to all of them. Not all of them whom he had chosen have, despite the appearance to the contrary, really chosen him. The situation among the disciples confirmed scripture, where it is written: "He that eateth bread with me hath lifted up his heel against me" (13:18; compare Psalm 41:9). There was a traitor even among the Twelve.

Peter wanted to know who he was. Peter was not in a position to ask without involving the entire group in coversation. So he motioned to another disciple next to Jesus to obtain the information. That other disciple was at Jesus' right, with his head reclining on the Master's chest, for he was "the disciple whom Jesus loved." Even our Lord, in his humanity, was, like us, discriminating in the degree of his affection among his friends and felt closer to one than he did to the others.

At a meal in those days among the Jews, the host's best friend was at the right of him at table, while the place to his left was reserved for the honored guest. Presumably Judas had this place, since he was sopping out of the same bowl as Jesus. Perhaps his position as treasurer of the group entitled him to such recognition. Poor Peter was across the table, probably in the end position. Perhaps Jesus put him there to test his humility. Given Peter's disposition, he might have been one of those examples in Jesus' teaching who invited himself to the chief place at table and had to be asked by his divine host to give way to another. Young John, by tradition, is identified as that "disciple whom Jesus loved." If Peter had been placed last, he would have been too far away to converse privately with Jesus and yet in clear view to signal across the table to John.

Two small pieces of information in John's account of the Last Supper indicate that it was celebrated as the Passover meal, even though it was eaten twenty-four hours or more before the beginning of Passover. Jesus and the disciples were eating in a reclining position, and they were supping together out of bowls where at least two or three would use the same bowl. This was the custom for the eating of Passover, the etiquette of which was different from that of ordinary meals.

Jesus said in response to John's inquiry as to who the traitor was, "He it is, to whom I shall give a sop, when I have dipped it" (13:26). After saying that quietly to John, so that no one else heard, he took a morsel of bread, dipped it into the bowl, and gave it to Judas. Judas knew what it meant, for Satan entered into him and inflamed his treachery. This is the only time John uses the word "Satan," or "adversary," in his Gospel (13:27). Judas also realized that Jesus knew what his intentions were, for when Jesus told him to do what he planned to do quickly, he got up from the table and left the room.

The other disciples thought Jesus had sent him on an errand, probably to buy food for the feast or to make some special donation to the poor. What does "the feast" mean? Were the disciples expecting another Passover observance at the proper time the next night? This is a puzzle. The only reason for celebrating it early would have been an impending emergency which would have prevented their being together at the regular time. The disciples did not know it. The emergency, of course, would be the crucifixion.

Speculation is that the upper room Jesus borrowed for the Passover meal with the disciples was the guest room in the home of a prominent Essene. The Essenes celebrated Passover a day ahead of the other Jews, and the traditional site of the upper room is located in what has been discovered to be the Essene district of New Testament Jerusalem. Archaeologists have uncovered the Essene Gate of the City, and it is only a few hundred yards from the upper room.

When Judas left, Jesus spoke of his impending glorification, associating thereby the shame of the cross with divine vindication. Then he gave the disciples the supreme commandment, which really was no commandment at all. How could love be commanded? Love was the gracious gift he had brought to them and which would be bestowed on them through the glory of his crucifixion. They were to love one another even as he had loved them.

Jesus called them "little children" (13:33). This is the only time this appellation is used in the Fourth Gospel. Note that Jesus used it when he told them that he would be with them on earth only a short time. He would go away, and they wouldn't be able to go with him.

Peter couldn't accept this. He protested that he would never let Jesus leave him but that he would follow him even to death. But Jesus smiled and said that the next morning before the cock crows Peter would have denied him three times.

Under stress, one who really loves the person he adores and serves can defect. The immediate result is the same as the defection of a traitor. But true love brings the defector back to his beloved. Peter came back to be the prince of apostles, Jesus' greatest and most effective convert. Judas hanged himself.

CHAPTER SEVEN

THE INCARNATE TRUTH

John 14:1–17:26

MATTHEW COLLECTS THE main body of Jesus' teachings in the Sermon on the Mount, in which Jesus teaches his new disciples on a small hill overlooking the Sea of Galilee.

John presents the teachings of our Lord in the form of discourses given to the disciples around the supper table in the upper room at the end of Jesus' last meal with them.

But the manner of the Johannine presentation is such that there is no clear discrimination between the words of Jesus and the thoughts of God which his words convey. Neither is there any clear distinction between the person speaking and his spoken words. Jesus exemplified in his own person the truth of what he declaimed.

For once in history, divine truth has clothed itself in the personality of a single, particular human being. Jesus was Truth talking about truth, just as he was the Way pointing out the way.

Assurance (14:1–15)

The eleven were disconsolate. They had come together with their master to enjoy a sumptuous meal in anticipation of the celebration of the Passover that would begin a night hence. But the meal turned out to be as lugubrious as a funeral wake. The disciples learned in the course of it that one of them was a traitor, that the most prominent of them would deny that he ever knew their teacher, and that the teacher would leave them never to return. Even Jesus himself had confessed that he was troubled, sore of heart, and depressed in spirit.

But then he reassured them. There was no reason for them to be upset. It was only natural for them to be sad over losing him, but he was just going a little ahead of them to prepare them a permanent place in God's own heavenly abode.

There is some difficulty in the expression "the Father's house of many mansions," so that some translations substitute "rooms" for "mansions." I don't think this substitute is a good translation of the Greek, nor do I think it is adequate to Jesus' meaning. Some scholars say that when a young Jew in that day got married, he brought his bride back to a home he himself had built for her on his father's estate. The newlyweds did not live under the same roof with the husband's parents. They had a home of their own on the family estate. If the parents were rich, that home might be a mansion.

God is rich. Jesus is saying to his followers that in the household of his Father he will himself build each of them a mansion, and they will live right there in heaven with him. The troubles of this life will be dissipated in the joy of the life to come. Disconsolation will be displaced by consolation. Anguish, fear, and pain will be destroyed by serenity, confidence, and total well-being. His leaving will be a preparation for their coming.

The way to him they already know, for he has shown it to them. But Thomas objected. He says, "Lord, we do not even know where you are going. How can we know the way to get there?" Jesus says that his own life should be the pattern of theirs. If they follow his example, that will be the way for them. It will lead them into the Father's house. "I am the way, and the truth, and the life; no one comes to the Father, but by me. If you had known me, you would have known my Father also; henceforth you know him and have seen him" (14:6–7, RSV).

Philip broke in to say: "Show him to us then. If we can be shown God, we won't need to concern ourselves with anything more."

Jesus' response was, "If I have been with you as long as I have and you have known me intimately, how can you ask for anything more. You have had God with you all this time, and yet your request indicates that you have never recognized me for who and what I am." Jesus had been, all along, the walking embodiment of God. His word had been God's word and his deeds God's deeds. "If you can't believe that God is acting in me, at least try to accept me on the basis of the value of the works I have performed." The ultimate proof of Christianity lies in what it changes.

Jesus assured the eleven that they will be able to carry on his work on earth for him, and the very things he has done they also will do, and even greater things than these because of his departure to the Father. The reason was that, when they ask something in his name, he will come himself to perform through them what they request. To evoke the name of Christ is to effect his nature as well as his power in the performance of what is prayed for. The Christian cannot pray for anything contrary to the nature and purpose of Christ. *To pray in his name is to want what he wants*. We cannot love him without keeping his commandments. To disobey Christ is to abandon our love for him. He promises to do anything we ask him to do if we ask it in his name, which means that what we ask must be an expression of his nature, not our own.

The destiny of all true disciples is to be with the Father by living with Jesus a life in keeping with his very own.

The Holy Spirit (14:16–31)

The source of assurance is the Holy Spirit, whom Jesus promised the disciples will take his place in their lives after he had gone from them. The Spirit will do for them everything that Jesus has done. He will be their counselor and comforter and will enable them to discern truth. Jesus had dwelt among them as another human being in their midst and has dealt with them as friend to friend. But the divine Presence will enter each one of their lives and will make his abode in their hearts and personalities. Jesus' stay had been temporary. He was about to leave them. But the Holy Spirit will stay with them forever. His presence will separate them from all others. That presence will give them their distinctiveness. Secular society will be entirely different from them and they from it, because that society will not possess the Spirit and so will not be able to understand or appreciate his ways. The eleven and all other followers of Jesus will always be segregated spiritually from the rest of humankind. And the instrument of such segregation is the divine Presence. The Holy Spirit is God living inside his own people.

Jesus was about to leave the eleven, and they knew it. But then Jesus promised that he would come back to them, implying thereby that he himself would be their comforter. This does not mean that this will take place at the end of time. He said it will be in a little while. On the surface, this refers to our Lord's post-resurrection experiences. But it also has a more permanent meaning, for even the post-resurrection experiences are short lived. What he means is that the comfort of the Holy Spirit is his comfort as well. God has but one nature; so the work of the Holy Spirit is the work of Father and Son as well. The Holy Spirit will call to remembrance all that Jesus himself taught and did during his earthly sojourn. "As long as you love me," Jesus tells them, "I will manifest myself to you. But that manifestation will be to you and other followers who love me, and to you and them alone." One of the disciples, Judas, but not Judas Iscariot, asked how Jesus could display himself to them and not to everybody else. Jesus' answer was that this manifestation will not be public. He and the Father will through the Holy Spirit, display themselves inwardly to those in whose lives they abide, and they will abide only with them who observe and keep the truth Jesus has taught them. The Greek word for "manifest" is unique in the New Testament to this chapter of John (14:21), and its meaning is quite different from the other words for "manifest" in the rest of the Bible. It is not a theophany as it is in the Old Testament but a personal experience.

The disciples will lose Jesus and yet keep him at the same time. Therefore, they should rejoice. He told them that if they really loved him, they could not help but rejoice, for he would again be with his Father who is greater than he. This does not mean that there are degrees of power and glory in the Godhead and that the Son is less in majesty than the

Father. It means that the Son will soon shed the impotence of his humanity and regain the omnipotence of his divinity and be back with the Father who has guided and protected him while he lived as a human being on earth. He warned them against the prince of this world and all the secularistic, materialistic, and atheistic influences that militate through evil against them. These powers have never had and can never have any control over him.

The disciples' hope of rescue from evil and its power is in keeping the commandments God gave him and he has given to them. The Holy Spirit will enable them to do so through the divine power and love dwelling in them.

The Disciples (15:1–25)

The transition from chapter 14 to chapter 15 in the Fourth Gospel is puzzling. The puzzle has nothing to do with the inspiring content of the two chapters, but rather with their arrangement. At the end of chapter 14, Jesus said, "Arise, let us go hence" (14:31). But four chapters later the reader discovers the same departure: "When Jesus had spoken these words, he went forth with his disciples over the brook Cedron, where was a garden, into the which he entered, and his disciples" (18:1). Where or when were the words in chapters 15 through 17 spoken? The last line of chapter 14 and the first sentence of chapter 18 must go together.

This problem has led some scholars to suggest that the material in this part of the Gospel of John is out of order. They insist chapters 15 through 17 must be placed before chapter 14 if chapter 14 concludes the table talk Jesus had with the disciples at the Last Supper. But to do this destroys the progression of thought in the discourse; the material does not make sense when rearranged. The trouble the disciples were experiencing was occasioned by their fear of losing Jesus. This is the reason for the assurance he gave them. And the cause of that assurance is the Holy Spirit, whom he promised them. Only after such assurance was he in a position to talk with them about themselves and give them the confidence and courage to face the hardships that will befall them.

What happened was probably that Jesus said, "Get ready. We must go now," but continued to talk to them, so that he talked as long after his suggestion that they start to leave as he had before. This is unusual with us in our hurried Western world. It was the usual practice in the leisurely Eastern world of the first century.

Jesus likened himself to a vine and the disciples to its branches, while God the Father is pictured as the farmer who cultivates the vineyard. The Father keeps the vine up on its trellis. He waters and tends the soil, so that the vine is properly nourished. He takes pride in his grapes. But this means that he also prunes the vine and removes the dead branches from it. The grapes hang on the branches. Dead branches bear no fruit. The analogy is plain. The disciples derive their life and strength from Jesus. If they break away from him, they are unproductive and die and have to be destroyed like broken branches on a grapevine.

Israel is often pictured in prophetic literature as a vine. She is the vine of God. Jesus himself as a new vine will be the new Israel of God. His new community, the Church, is the continuation in history of his very self, giving the fruit of his redemption to the world. This new community expresses itself and does its work through its members, the first of whom are the original disciples. Whatever fruit they bear is a result of their labors. But they cannot do anything apart from Jesus. Only as they keep his commandments and display his love, each for the other, and also for the world they are sent to save, can they remain his disciples and carry out to success the mission he has given them. They must imitate Jesus in everything. They must shirk no hardship. They must be willing if necessary to die for his cause. "Remember the word that I said unto you, The servant is not greater than his lord" (15:20).

Some will hate them just as they hated Jesus, and they will persecute them just as they persecuted Jesus. But others will hear and receive them as they themselves heard and received Jesus. The success they have in winning people to Jesus' cause and making them disciples like themselves will be their love. True love in the end is sacrificial: "Greater love hath no man than this, that a man lay down his life for his friends'' (15:13). That is what Jesus was doing for them. He no longer called them servants or even pupils. They were his friends. He treated them as equals. He loved them more than he loved himself. Everything the Father has told him he has shared with them.

However, they must be prepared for rejection. Just as the secular world rejected him, it will reject them, too. People who hated Jesus will hate his followers. In hating Jesus and his followers, they hate God as well, for all Jesus did was in compliance with God's commandment. The paradox of life is that often those we do the most for turn out to be our worst enemies. Jesus quoted to his disciples a messianic prophecy from the Old Testament: ''They hated me without a cause'' (15:25; compare Psalm 35:19; 69:4).

Witness (15:26–16:33)

Likewise, the followers of Jesus can expect similar treatment from the very people they attempt most to help and to save. The business of the disciples is to witness to Jesus. The eleven had been trained by their master to do this, since they had been with him since the very beginning of his ministry. He handpicked them for the task. He had been their living example. Even so, the Holy Spirit, who will be to them both comfort and truth, will enhance their witness by his own, for he, too, will testify to Jesus and the validity of his work.

Jesus told his disciples what to expect from society, so that they would not be surprised when disaster befell them. They were all Jews. But the Jews would expel them from the synagogues. It was customary then to exclude a person from the synagogue for a month if that person criticized the religious authorities. If a person's offense against the Jewish religion was great enough, such a one might be denied admission to the synagogue for as long as six months. Though rare, excommunication might take place when the offender was excluded from synagogue and temple for an indefinite period of time. This latter state might be the disciples' fate for promoting the teachings of an executed criminal. Indeed, they might as well expect death itself, for the Jewish religious leaders would think they themselves were fulfilling the will of God in executing followers of the Galilean they were about to execute. People would do these things to the followers of Jesus, because they would never come themselves to know Jesus and the Father who sent him.

Our Lord told the eleven that he could appreciate the sorrow they felt in losing him. But really they would be better off now without him, because his departure from them would precipitate the coming of the Holy Spirit. The Holy Spirit not only would comfort them and enable them to know the truth but also would comfort the world and possess the power not to be overcome by the world.

The Spirit's mission to the world is threefold:

● The Holy Spirit will convict people of sin. The root of sin is the failure to recognize and accept Jesus Christ as both the way to God and the truth about God.

● The Holy Spirit will convince people of the rightness of God. He will lead them to see the inadequacy of their own standards of behavior by showing them God's purpose for his creation and for them as his creatures.

● The Holy Spirit will bring them to judgment. By him they will be brought to accountability. They will be judged by God in compliance with his disclosure of himself in Jesus Christ.

Therefore, the disciples need not lose confidence nor despair, for the victory of the Holy Spirit over the world will be their victory, too. They will share in triumph.

In the meantime, the divine Presence will be their support and strength. Jesus' earthly stay with them was too short. He did not have time to teach them all he wanted them to know. But, as occasion arises, the Holy Spirit will enable them to discern the truth. And they will find that everything the Holy Spirit teaches them will revolve around him and point toward him, because everything the Father has he has given to the Son and the Son shares equally with the Father. The Holy Spirit does not initiate; the Spirit confirms. The Comforter does not add anything new to the teachings of

Jesus. His mission is to enable people to see the validity of what Jesus taught and to appropriate his message as their own. More than all else, the divine Presence empowers believers to live as Jesus lived.

At this point in the discourse, Jesus introduced a paradox. He said that in a little while they will not see him. And yet in a little while they will see him. They are befuddled by this contradiction. How can they not see him and yet see him?

The only explanation he gives is that he is going to his Father. But that reason is the answer to their question. The crucifixion will take him from them, seemingly forever. Death erects an insurmountable barrier. But the resurrection will restore him to them. They will see him in his post-resurrection appearances. When he goes back to the Father, he will regain the divine attributes he had before he became a human being. He will possess once more the Father's omnipresence.

The disciples will be able, after the return of their master to heaven, to ask anything in his name and receive what they ask for. It has never occurred to them heretofore to ask God for anything in Jesus' name, for Jesus has been with them, in simple fellowship. But, when he is gone, they will know the true relationship that has always existed between him and the Father. They will realize the Father himself loves them because they love his son.

These things will take place subsequently. But right then, that very night, the disciples would desert him and go back to their homes. Jesus wouldn't have anyone to support him. Yet he would have all the support in the whole of creation, for the Father was with him.

In losing him, the disciples would go through the pain of childbirth. But in recovering him in his divine existence, they would experience the joy of the mother in her newborn child. Jesus assured his disciples of power. The power would come through the trials and tribulations the world would inflict on them. Still they need not be disturbed. Their master, they will know by his living presence, has overcome and defeated the world.

The High Priestly Prayer (17:1–26)

Naturally, Jesus ended his discourse with his disciples after the supper in the upper room with prayer. The prayer he prayed is the longest prayer recorded in the four Gospels. Though the synoptics indicate that he prayed often, what he said in those prayers is generally by them left unrecorded. In most instances he had withdrawn from them and was alone; so they did not hear what he said. The exceptions were the Lord's Prayer, which Matthew and Luke record, and a few others, which are very short, consisting only of a sentence or two, such as the prayer in the Garden of Gethsemane before his arrest.

This prayer, like the Lord's Prayer, is a public utterance, albeit that the public in both cases is limited to the disciples. Nonetheless it has liturgical significance.

The nature of the prayer is priestly. Its purpose is the same as that of the prayer the high priest would make on the Day of Atonement, when the ram was driven out into the wilderness with the sins of the people symbolically on its back. The Lamb of God is about to be offered up for the sins of the world. This is his prayer of consecration. He is both the high priest and also the sacrifice which the high priest offers to God.

The prayer is liturgical. It is a pattern for the disciples to use in the future as is the Lord's Prayer. We do not say it by rote in services of worship as we do the Lord's Prayer. But we observe its principles when we pray, and its structure has dictated that of subsequent prayers through the centuries. It is instruction for worship, because it teaches theology, as well as inspires devotion.

The high priestly prayer begins, as does the Lord's Prayer, in adoration and praise. It ascribes glory to God. But it does this in an entirely different way than does the Lord's Prayer. Jesus himself prays the Father to glorify him, his son, in order that he may glorify the Father. He acknowledges that the Father has already glorified him on earth through the mission he has enabled him to perform, and now he asks the Father to lend him his own glory, or rather to give him back the glory he had before his incarnation, the glory he possessed from the foundation of the world.

What does this mean? It means that Jesus Christ is divine. When we pray to God, we also pray to Christ, because he has shared deity with the Father throughout all eternity. The glory of God is the glory of both the Father and the son.

Therefore, the very ascription of glory to the Father is also a petition that that same glory will be manifested in the son, as it has been already by the son to the disciples whom the Father has given him. Since this is a priestly prayer, it is prayed in intercession for the disciples. Jesus asks the Father to keep them in unity with him and with one another as he and the Father are in perfect unity with each other. Jesus prayed the Father to keep the disciples as he himself kept them while he was with them on earth. He does not ask the Father to deliver them out of the world with its bad influences but to protect them from evil as they live and serve in the world. Jesus prays God to sanctify the disciples, so that they might be a sanctifying influence in the world. Like the high priest, who sanctifies himself in the manner prescribed by Moses, in order to represent the needs of the people to God, Jesus sanctifies himself in order that through his priestly service and sacrifice, his disciples might be sanctified. He thanks the Father for having kept them intact. Only one has forsaken him.

The prayer closes with a petition for all humankind. Jesus prays the Father to make the disciples one, as he and the Father are one, so that through their ministry together the world might believe on him and know that God the Father has sent him. The absolute unity that exists between Father and son must likewise exist among the followers of Jesus if they are to carry out their mission and thereby bring salvation in the name of Jesus to the whole world. The purpose of our Lord's mission on earth has been to declare God's will and to make possible for all people the love the Father has had for him. He wants humankind to share in that love, and his desire is to dwell in them as the Father has dwelt in him.

CHAPTER EIGHT

THE INCARNATE GOD

John 18:1–20:31

EVERYTHING JOHN HAS written up to now is preface to the great event of our Lord's death and resurrection. The six miracles he has presented are but signs pointing to the one great miracle of the sacrifice that effects redemption and destroys death in resurrection. In John's perspective, what happens on Calvary and what takes place afterwards in Joseph of Arimathea's tomb are not two events, separate and distinct from one another, but a single act in the divine drama of salvation. Death is not the obverse of life but only a passing phase of its endless continuity. The crucifixion is not tragedy that must be overcome by the resurrection but rather stands together with resurrection as God's victory over evil and his conquest of sin.

Therefore, in the Johannine perspective, it is not appropriate to speak of our Lord's passion. Jesus is not so much acted on and mistreated by the hands of evil people as he is active in using the deeds of sinners to manifest God's glory and at the same time to bring about their salvation.

In the earlier parts of the Fourth Gospel, as we have shown by the titles to the various chapters of this book, John has delineated some essential characteristics of God in his revelation of himself in his son, such as Word, Deed, Light, Life, Way, and Truth. Jesus has incarnated and therefore manifested in human form and behavior the great attributes of the omnipotent and everlasting God. But now in this chapter, he reveals the full personality and character of God. He shows himself to be God in human form. He is what God would be if God became a human being. And he is that because God did become a real historical person in him. John presents Jesus of Nazareth as the incarnate God. ''Now is the Son of man glorified, and God is glorified in him. If God be glorified in him, God shall also glorify him in himself, and shall straightway glorify him'' (13:31–32). ''(And we beheld his glory, the glory as of the only begotten of the Father,) full of grace and truth'' (1:14). ''No man hath seen God at any time; the only begotten Son, which is in the bosom of the Father, he hath declared him'' (1:18).

Arrest and Interrogation by the Jewish Authorities (18:1–27)

After prayer with the disciples at the conclusion of his table talk in the upper room, Jesus descended with them from Mount Zion, crossed the Kidron (Cedron) Valley, and entered a garden on the lower slopes of the Mount of Olives. The Kidron is a wadi, a small stream of running water in the rainy season but usually a dry bed of sand and stones. John does not name the garden, but says that it was a place to which Jesus frequently repaired with the disciples. No doubt, before Judas left the meal, arrangements had been made for the little group to convene after supper at its customary meeting place for prayer before crossing over the Mount of Olives to Bethany to spend the night.

No sooner had Jesus and the disciples entered the garden than Judas arrived with a band of soldiers, including officers whom he had procured from the chief priests and the Pharisees. This band must have been from the Temple guard, an entirely Jewish constabulary force which protected the Temple and enforced its ritualistic regulations and functioned under orders from the high priest.

How large was it? ''Band'' might refer to a Roman cohort, which numbered six hundred men, or it might mean a maniple, which was a unit of two hundred men. To say the least, Jesus was captured by a host of enemies. The guards came equipped not just with lanterns but lighted torches as well. They thought they might have to hunt him down, perhaps surrounded by his army, among the trees and bushes on the mountainside.

Instead, he came out to them and asked them whom they sought. Immediately, he identified himself to them. He did not wait for Judas to point him out. The power and magnetism of his personality was such that it repelled arrest. The professional soldiers realized the enormity of their guilt, in executing the orders the chief priests had given them in apprehending Jesus. They drew back and fell on their faces before him. In describing this, John impresses on us the regal character of our Lord even as he suffered the indignity of being apprehended as a criminal. The spontaneous response of the Temple guard in prostrating themselves before Jesus was a token of his deity, even though those who paid him homage were not aware of what they had done. Perhaps all of this happened before the treacherous kiss of Judas, mentioned by the other three evangelists.

John, alone of the Gospel writers, tells us that Jesus was willing to submit to the guards if they would consent to let his disciples go. This was in fulfillment of what he had said to the Father in his high priestly prayer: "Of those whom thou gavest me I lost not one" (18:9, RSV; 17:12). It was also essential that they remain free if his life and work were to be remembered and if the Church, his new Israel, was to be formed. Jesus' turning himself over to the guards bought for the disciples their freedom. Jesus bought their life with his death.

But Peter was not willing for Jesus to surrender himself without resistance to the guards. He wanted to put up a fight. And fight he did, for he drew his sword and struck the servant of the high priest and cut off his right ear. At this point, John supplies two details that the synoptic writers miss. He tells us who it was that struck the servant. When the other evangelists wrote their Gospels, Peter was still alive, and it might have endangered him to supply this information. Peter was dead when John wrote his Gospel. But John also supplies the name of the person whom Peter injured. His name was Malchus. Evidently John knew his name when the others did not.

Jesus told Peter to sheathe his sword. This ordeal had been permitted by God. Was it not his duty to accept it and undergo it? He calls it his "cup" that he must drink (18:11). He uses similar language here that the synoptic writers report he used when he prayed in the Garden of Gethsemane that this cup might pass from him, but not his will but God's will be done (Matt. 26:39, Mark 14:36; Luke 22:42). With that, the guards bound him and led him away as if he were a common criminal.

Jesus was not taken directly to Caiaphas, the high priest, but was carried to the house of Annas, Caiaphas' father-in-law. Annas had served as high priest from A.D. 6 to 15. Peter and another disciple, not named, followed along after Jesus and his captors. The Johannine narrative is not clear as to whether the interrogation took place at the home of Annas or of Caiaphas. It states the high priest asked Jesus certain questions. But that still might well have been applied loosely to Annas as well as Caiaphas, as we still address former presidents of the United States as "Mr. President" even though another now occupies the office.

What we know is that the unnamed disciple was permitted to enter the house, while Peter was detained outside. The other disciple was known to the high priest. Probably this unnamed disciple was John, for John through his mother was related to Elizabeth, the mother of John the Baptist. Elizabeth was a descendant of Aaron. That could account for John's knowing the name of the high priest's servant. This would be further evidence that John, the son of Zebedee, wrote the Fourth Gospel.

No matter, this unnamed disciple got Peter admitted, and the serving maid accused him as he entered of being a disciple, too. This relationship Peter denied.

Jesus' priestly interlocutor, either Annas or Caiaphas, asked but two questions. One question was about Jesus' disciples, and the other, about his doctrine or teachings. Jesus told him he could get this information better from his listeners. Then it was that an officer slapped him for being impertinent to the high priest.

Jesus was but observing the nicety of the law. Rabbinic law relieved one of giving evidence that might incriminate himself. Jesus but asserted his rights when he asked the officer if he had said anything inadmissible as evidence in a Jewish court. Why should he be called impertinent by declining to supply information which rabbinic law itself forbade the authorities to wheedle out of an accused person?

Peter had been standing warming himself before the fire when a maid said, "Aren't you one of his disciples?"

Peter said, "No."

Then a servant akin to Malchus, whose ear Peter had severed, said, "Didn't I see you in the garden with him?" Peter was afraid this person would connect him with the crime he had committed against Malchus. He denied again that he even knew Jesus. He had but followed, like the rest, out of curiosity. At this point, the dawn broke and the cock began to crow. Peter, who had so boldly tried to defend Jesus in the garden and who at the Last Supper had declared he would die for his master, now realized that he could not save Jesus. He desperately needed somebody to save him. He did not realize it then, but that somebody would be Jesus, whom he had denied.

John makes it clear in this part of his narrative that, both at his arrest in the garden and at his interrogation by the high priest, Jesus is still in control of the situation. The guards who arrested him were appalled at his majesty. And his authority and mastery of rabbinic law are superior to the high priest's who judged him. His behavior throughout this ordeal was divine.

The Roman Trial (18:28–19:16)

If not noted for compassion and mercy, Rome was, at least, recognized for its justice. The term "Roman justice" is legendary. When we use it, we mean a person gets exactly what that person deserves. Rome, more than any other state in antiquity, gave to the world law and order. Therefore, the subjects of her conquered provinces preferred to be judged by Rome than by their own local authorities. This procedure was not always possible. One had to be either a Roman citizen, as in the case of Paul, or else guilty of a crime against the empire rather than an infraction of a provincial or racial law over which the recognized authorities among the conquered people had the right of judgment.

In the trial of Jesus, however, even justice was subverted. The subversion, odd as it may seem, came not from his Roman judge but from his Jewish accusers, that is, his own race and his own people. The Roman judge was able to secure and properly to assess the evidence and on the basis of it to render a just verdict. Pilate gave Jesus a fair trial. In it, we see a clear and unimpeachable example of Roman justice. But we also see a pitiful example of the inability of Rome in this instance to apply the justice she had so correctly perceived. Political pressure from the conquered overpowered the justice of the conqueror. Pilate in Jerusalem fell under the control of the people he had been sent out by Rome to control.

The Roman capital of the province of Judea was Caesarea. In that city by the Mediterranean Sea, the procurator lived. The Jewish capital, of course, was Jerusalem, with its Temple and the Sanhedrin or governing assembly. The Roman procurator came to Jerusalem only on special occasions, generally when a riot or political demonstration was expected. On such occasions he lent his presence and that of his soliders to preserve law and order and to assert the authority of Rome. The Passover was one of those occasions, for this the supreme religious feast of the Jews was also the most dangerous time of the year. Disorder and violence were more apt to break out at Passover than at any other time. The Jews' remembrance of their delivery from slavery in Egypt in the long ago made them anxious to throw off the Roman yoke and become once again an independent nation.

Therefore, the Sanhedrin wanted to take advantage of this situation. By accusing Jesus of being a political agitator and threat to law and order, they expected to induce Pilate to execute him. If a riot ensued, the blame for it would not be on them (they knew how popular Jesus was with the people) but on the Roman procurator who sentenced him. Rome could not blame them for a sentence her own agent had rendered.

The examination of Jesus by the high priest and presumably the Sanhedrin had lasted all night, so he was taken shortly after daybreak to Pilate's "hall of judgment" (18:28), the Antonia, which was a Roman fortress as well as seat of government in Jerusalem. This is where the procurator stayed when he was in the city.

"Early" as used in the Gospel is a technical term. The last two watches of the night were "cockcrow" and "early." Peter's denial had taken place at "cockcrow," just before the breaking of the day. "Early" was daybreak itself. The Jewish authorities got to the Antonia with Jesus before 6:00 a.m. Pilate, no doubt, had to be awakened and brought out to them. Since this was the day of preparation for the Passover, which began at sunset, they would not go inside. They did not want to defile themselves by entering a gentile establishment. It is difficult to know why they were so precautious. They could have cleansed themselves and washed away all defilement by taking a hot bath at sunset. Maybe they would be too busy with Temple duties to have time for this. Whatever the reason, they stayed in the courtyard outside.

When Pilate asked them what the accusation was, they gave no specific charges other than the general complaint that Jesus was a malefactor. In the light of Pilate's examination of Jesus, the implication was that Jesus was an agitator against Rome. When Pilate told the chief priests to judge him by their own Law, they responded that capital punishment was not in their power to inflict but was reserved for Rome to administer. But later the Jews stoned Stephen to death and made him the first Christian martyr. Rome had no hand in that. And John himself tells how they were about to stone the woman caught in adultery. Their own Law prescribed that a person guilty of blasphemy be stoned to death. This is exactly what they had found Jesus guilty of (19:7). The Jews could not inflict crucifixion. This is the type death Jesus foretold he would encounter (18:32).

Pilate took Jesus inside and immediately asked him if he were the king of the Jews. Jesus, in response, asked him if he had heard this or did he discern it himself, implying thereby that it was true. Pilate said, "I am no Jew. How would I know one way or the other what you are? You are here before me simply because you have been accused by your own people.''

Jesus reassured him by saying that he was not in competition with him or any other earthly ruler. His kingdom was not of this world. But, when Pilate asked again if he were a king, Jesus admitted that he was, for he was born into the world to give regal witness to the truth. He ruled by the persuasion of great ideas, not by coercion and force. ''Every one that is of the truth [anyone who is sincerely interested in truth] heareth my voice'' (18:37).

Pilate sarcastically asked, ''What is truth?'', but he did not tarry for an answer. He went immediately back out to Jesus' accusers to say to them that he found no fault in the accused. If they did, however, and wanted him publicly to validate their judgment, he could do so and afterwards release Jesus according to the custom at Passover of pardoning and releasing a criminal chosen by the people. But they said they would not choose Jesus but Barabbas, a convicted robber.

Pilate did all he knew to save Jesus from death and, at the same time, to satisfy the Jews. He allowed his soldiers to scourge him, a punishment next to death. When one was scourged, his body was lashed with whips impregnated with nails. Many died under the ordeal. The soldiers mocked him by pressing a crown of thorns on his head and putting a royal purple robe around him. Then he led him back to the Jews in the courtyard. ''Look now,'' he said, ''this is your king! What power has he? What can he do to harm anybody? He is weak and helpless! Isn't this punishment enough? Let him go! I find no crime that he has committed against anybody, much less Rome!'' The Jews then reminded Pilate of their law against blasphemy. They said that Jesus had called himself the son of God.

John says at this point Pilate appeared to be very much afraid. Why? It may have been that he was superstitious. Maybe, he thought, the Jews also worship a real god with real power. It could be, in the light of all this man has done, he is that god's son. If so, he did not want to endanger himself by mistreating him.

So he took Jesus back inside to the judgment hall. He asked him outright who he really was and where he came from, but Jesus decided to remain silent. He felt he had said enough. Then Pilate reminded him that he had the power of life and death over him. He implied that it would be in his interest to speak up. Jesus' reply but enhanced Pilate's fear of him, for he said that Pilate had no power other than the power God permitted him to wield. So Pilate tried all the more to win the consent of the Jews to release Jesus.

Why was he so eager to please the people whom he ruled and also despised? What advantage was there to him in this? In this instance, he was afraid of them, because Jesus had admitted to being a king and the Jews had said publicly that he had cast himself, by that declaration, in rivalry with Caesar. The Jews had influence in Rome. If they could convince Caesar that Pilate had been lax in protecting the name, title, and honor of the emperor, then he would certainly be recalled and perhaps even condemned and executed. In the end, his fear of the misrepresentation of the Jews and the bad effect it might have on his relationship with the emperor was greater than his superstitious fear of Jesus or his duty as a judge to administer justice. Therefore, he sat down in the judgment seat in the courtyard of the Antonia on what was called "the Pavement" (19:13). We do not know exactly what "pavement" means. We know from Josephus that the courtyard of the Antonia was an area paved with tiles. But we also know that the procurators carried with them for purposes of rendering judgment a piece of pavement large enough to hold a chair in which they sat. This is probably what "pavement" refers to in the Fourth Gospel.

Once again Pilate asked, "Shall I crucify your king?"

When the Jews answered, "We have no king but Caesar" (19:15), Pilate gave in to them and pronounced the sentence of crucifixion on Jesus.

As at his arrest and interrogation before the high priest, so again at this Roman trial, Jesus displayed his divine nature and was more authoritative and in command of himself than was his Roman judge. Indeed, it looks from start to end as if he were the judge and Pilate the person under examination.

When Pilate asked him if he were the king of the Jews, he said that if his kingdom had been political, his followers would have resisted his arrest by force and he would not have fallen into the hands of the Jewish leaders. When Pilate threatened him, he said calmly that Pilate had no authority but by divine providence and that the God who permitted him to exercise it could take it from him at will. The clear implication is that Jesus who stands in judgment could and in the end would judge his own judge. Even Pilate's sentence and the death penalty were dependent upon Jesus' willingness to undergo it and his divine permission for it to be carried out. Here is God in the form of a man allowing himself to be tried, condemned, and put to death by sinners, his own creatures who have rebelled against their creator. Pilate's words, "Behold the man" (19:5) have a meaning for us beyond his intention: "Behold the God!"

The Crucified Savior (19:17–42)

John's account of the crucifixion is more compressed than the accounts of the other three evangelists and shorter than theirs. He omits many important historical details such as the conscription of a bystander to carry Jesus' cross for him after he had stumbled and fallen, the confession of the Roman centurion, and Jesus' assurance of salvation to the penitent thief. Likewise, he makes no reference to the darkness in midafternoon, the rending of the veil of the Temple, or the parade of the dead through the streets, so vividly described by Matthew. John is selective rather than comprehensive in what he reports about the crucifixion.

He implies that Jesus bore his cross all the way to *Golgotha*, the Hebrew word for "skull." The place of the skull may have gotten its name from the fact that it was the hill for executions or maybe its geographical appearance was that of a skull. "Gordon's Calvary" (the place General Gordon identified as the site of the crucifixion) looks exactly like a skull with a ridge for a nose and two huge indentations on either side of the ridge that look like eye sockets. John says that Jesus' cross stood between the crosses of two others who were crucified with him, but he does not identify them as malefactors (perhaps insurrectionists), as does Luke.

He gives the inscription Pilate affixed to Jesus' cross. It was customary to put the name of the criminal and the crime for which he was given the death sentence on his cross. The crime Pilate affixed was "King of the Jews." The Jews complained that he was not their king, but an imposter who claimed to be their king. Pilate refused to alter what he had written.

This crime guaranteed to Rome that Pilate had rendered justice in his sentence. Death was the only penalty that could be inflicted on one who made himself the ruler of a subjugated province of the empire and thereby threatened revolt leading to independence. But if he were a Jewish king, he had to have Jewish subjects who followed him. The Jews thought this inscription might implicate them in Jesus' crime. Pilate, in protecting himself, might endanger them. But to John there is "poetic justice" in the inscription. Pilate was confirming Jesus' regal status without knowing what he was doing, and the Jews were having it inflicted on them against their wills. In John's mind, there was irony in this title, for these mocking words were the truth.

The evangelist reports that the title was written in Hebrew, Greek, and Latin, here again, without Pilate's realizing it or the Jews' accepting it, indicating the universality of Jesus' kingship. The man on the cross was king of the Jews, who rejected him, and king of the Romans, who sentenced him to death, and king of the Greeks, too, though they had never heard of him. This title, or inscription, promised that eventually every knee will bow to Jesus as king whether it wants to or not.

John says that the soldiers divided his garments among them but cast lots for his coat because it was without seams and was too valuable to be cut up into pieces. John says that this is in fulfillment of an Old Testament prophecy (Psalm 22:18). Psalm 22 is one of the messianic psalms. Subtly the fourth evangelist uses this reference to indicate that the people were killing their own Messiah. John also implies a connection between the coat of Jesus and the tunic of the high priest. Aaron was instructed to come to the altar wearing it when he did sacrifice (Lev. 16:4). The Roman soldiers had at their disposal the tunic of the high priest who was offering himself as the sacrifice for the sins of the whole world.

There were just four Roman soldiers sent to carry out the crucifixion. This was the prescribed mode for such executions. It is evident by this time neither Pilate nor the Jewish leaders expected a riot. People lost interest in Jesus when they thought he had lost his power to accommodate their wants.

John is the only evangelist to preserve the charge that Jesus gave to the son of Zebedee to look after his mother. By this, he showed that there was at least one disciple with him when he died. There is no evidence whatever that the others, even Peter, were present. John names three women who came there: the mother and aunt of Jesus and Mary Magdalene. The synoptics supply names of others (Mark 15:40; Matt. 27:55–56). Could it be that John mentions this charge that Jesus gave to the young disciple to care for his mother because that disciple was the fourth evangelist himself?

When death was too slow in coming to people being crucified, the soldiers would come by and break their legs. This took from the victims what little support they had to hold themselves upright on their cross. It forced them to slouch down and thereby restricted their breathing, so that death ensued shortly therefrom. The Jews insisted that this be done, so that the victims might be removed and their bodies disposed of before the beginning of the sabbath at sunset. This the soldiers dutifully did on the other two condemned men. But it was unnecessary in Jesus' case, since he was already dead. A soldier, however, took a spear and pierced his side to make certain he had expired. From the wound flowed blood and water. In the mind of the evangelist as well as in that of the later church, this historical incident had more than historical significance. The water and the blood symbolize the cleansing power Jesus exerts in baptism and the property of everylasting life he confers through sacrifice, celebrated at holy communion. As in life, so in death, Jesus is still the incarnate God and merciful Savior.

John is careful to show that the burial of Jesus is that of a rich, powerful, and affluent person. He was put in a sepulcher that had never been used before. That sepulcher was in a garden near the skull, where he had been crucified. Its owner was the influential and affluent Joseph of Arimathea, a secret admirer and follower of Jesus, but who now openly claimed the body from Pontius Pilate.

The person who brought the mixture of myrrh and aloes was Nicodemus, a member of the Sanhedrin, who had come to consult Jesus at night early in Jesus' ministry. Myrrh and aloes blended together comprise the ointment commonly used by Jews to anoint the bodies of their dead. It is not what was used but the amount that is impressive. Nicodemus brought for the burial one hundred pounds worth of the mixture. That was enough to use on a great many bodies, but all of it was expended on Jesus. Jesus was wrapped in fine linens, and the mixture was poured on the body and between the linen wrappings. This prisoner, condemned as a malefactor, was given a burial as splendid as the burial of kings.

His last words had been: "It is finished" (19:30). He had been in command of himself to the very end. He did not have life wrested from him, though he had been crucified as a criminal. He freely laid it down. He had offered himself as the sacrifice for the sins of the whole world.

The fourth evangelist indicates that Jesus died in the middle of the afternoon on the day of the preparation for the Passover. He died at the very hour the lambs were being slain by the priests on the altar of the Temple in Jerusalem in preparation for the Passover meal that would begin at sunset. The lamb of Passover had to be without blemish, with no bones broken. So was this lamb, the Lamb of God, slain in the purpose of God from the foundation of the world.

"It is finished" meant more than the end of Jesus' earthly life. It meant also, and more poignantly, that the act of redemption had taken place, that the price of sin had all been paid, and that sinners before and since could be justified and counted as righteous before God. This theme is reflected in Charles Wesley's hymn"'Tis Finished! The Messiah Dies":

'Tis finished! The Messiah dies
Cut off for sins, but not his own,
Accomplished is the sacrifice;
The great redeeming work is done.

The Risen Lord (20:1–31)

In the synoptics, the discovery that the tomb in which Jesus had been laid was empty belongs exclusively to the women. In the Johannine narrative, this remarkable event is shared with two of the disciples, and only one woman is associated with them in the discovery. That woman is Mary Magdalene.

She came between the watches of "cockcrow" and "early" to the sepulcher and found the stone which sealed the tomb rolled back and the entrance open. This was the extent of her discovery. It was still dark. She was startled and afraid. She did not even look in. She ran to find Peter and "the other disciple whom Jesus loved" and told them what she had found. She assumed that the body of Jesus was no longer inside, for she added that it had been removed and she did not know where it had been placed. Since Jesus had had to be buried hurriedly before sunset when the sabbath began, it is probable that Joseph of Arimathea had just lent him his tomb temporarily and had intended to move him to another grave after the sabbath had passed. If so, the disciples would have fully expected to be informed of this and to help in the removal.

This other disciple whom Jesus loved was John. On receiving the news from Mary, the two ran to the sepulcher, and John, being younger, outran Peter and got there first. He waited for Peter before going in. When they entered, all they found were the grave clothes. These convinced them that something more than the removal of a body had taken place. If the body had been removed, it would have stayed wrapped in its burial clothes. Therefore, John "believed" (20:8). He realized that Jesus was what he said he was. He was the incarnate God.

The two men left. Mary alone remained. When she entered the sepulcher after their departure, two angels had come and taken their places at the head and foot of the tomb. During the time that the two disciples were inside, Mary had stayed in the garden weeping. She was still in tears as she entered the sepulcher. The angels asked her why she was weeping. As she answered them but before they could reply, she looked back and saw a man standing at the entrance to the sepulcher. Her eyes were too full of tears for her to do more than glance at him. He repeated the question of the angels. She took it for granted that he was the gardener and asked what he had done with the body of Jesus. But when he called her name, she knew for certain who he was. The sheep always know the voice of their shepherd. She cried out in joy, "Rabboni" (20:16). The word means "master," as the King James Version indicates. But it means more. *Rabbi* was the word for a teacher or master. *Rabboni* was used for God, the perfect or true teacher. Mary Magdalene, like John, recognized her earthly master as the incarnate God.

As she started to touch him, Jesus asked her to refrain, saying, "I have not yet gone up to my Father," implying that his condition was not as it was before the crucifixion but as it should forever be in company with his Father in heaven. He told Mary to go tell his "brethren," meaning the disciples, that he was on his way to his Father and their Father. This is the first time that Jesus referred to his disciples as his brothers. Yes, and the first message the risen Lord gave to anyone to deliver in his name he entrusted to a woman. Mary Magdalene is the first person after the resurrection to announce the Christian gospel to the world.

The risen Lord reappeared at nightfall to visit with the disciples in Jerusalem. To the Jews, this was another day, since their day began at sunset; and so it was to the disciples at this time. But John is writing from Ephesus many years later. For him at the time of his writing, it was the evening of the same day (20:19). It was still the day of the resurrection. The Christian reckoning of time had displaced the Jewish.

The disciples were behind locked doors for fear of the Jews. Yet Jesus came to them without knocking. He stood among them, though they had not admitted him. He was recognizable. He had his same body with the nail prints and the wound in his side. But now his body was no encumbrance. It adjusted to his will. What he did was no longer limited by it. In this appearance, he shows us what life is like in heaven. We will all be recognizable! We will have our personalities. But we won't be limited by our physical bodies any more.

Jesus gave the disciples their commission to witness to him. He sent them forth to the world as the Father had sent him to them. And he breathed on them and thereby gave them the gift of the Holy Spirit. Just as God breathed into man and woman the breath of life at creation, so Jesus gave spiritual life by breathing on believers. They received the Holy Spirit, which is his spirit as well.

Thomas was not present when this took place. He would not believe what the others had told him. So eight days later, Jesus came again to him. Our Lord made his appearance in the same manner as he had on the night of his resurrection. Thomas had said that he would not believe until he felt with his hands the nail prints and the open spear wound. So Jesus, before Thomas could ask, laid bare his wounds and insisted the doubter examine them. Thomas did not touch him but cried out in shame and, yet, in joy, "My Lord and my God." Thomas stated the first confession of the Christian church. Honest doubt is a necessary prelude to genuine faith.

It took the visible presence of Jesus to convince Thomas. But more blessed are we who do not have that visible presence but, through the enlightenment of the Holy Spirit, believe.

The crucified Savior is the risen Lord. The cross has become not just the instrument of shame on which a criminal died but the sword of victory over sin and the sole means to everlasting life.

As Charles Wesley wrote in the second verse of "And Should It Be That I Should Gain":

'Tis mystery all! th' Immortal dies!
Who can explore his strange design?
In vain the first-born seraph tries
To sound the depths of love divine.

'Tis mercy all! let earth adore;
Let angel minds inquire no more.

The incarnate God died for our sins on the cross. On the third day, he rose again from the dead and has opened thereby the gates of heaven to all believers. Jesus Christ is our Lord and Savior, God in human form.

CHAPTER NINE

THE EPILOGUE

John 21:1–25

AS JOHN BEGINS his Gospel with a prologue, so he ends it with an epilogue. The prologue, as we have seen, gives the reason for our Lord's advent and lays bare the doctrine of the incarnation. From it we know in advance of the narrative that follows *who* it is with whom we deal and the *purpose* of his coming. The epilogue gives the *result* of his coming and portrays his *continuing work* with his followers after his earthly sojourn in the flesh is over.

It serves, therefore, as a means of transition from the earthly career of Jesus to the beginning of the church and affirms his living presence among those who believe on him. The church, through her members, becomes the corporate successor to the person of Jesus. The church is his collective body which he guides and protects through his living spirit, always present within the church. As he saved humankind and blessed people wherever he found them, so will his disciples. Though not any more in the flesh, the risen Christ is present always to guide and strengthen them.

My caption for the epilogue is "The Living Christ."

It is significant that the disciples went back to Galilee. They had left Jerusalem. Their contact with the risen Lord was an inspiring memory. They were where most subsequent lay persons will be—hard at work at their trades. Peter said, "I go a fishing" (21:3), and he invited those on the shore with him to accompany him by fishing with him. Seven of the disciples were there. They got into the boat and put out to sea. But they didn't catch anything.

In the early morning when it was too dark to see, a

stranger called to them from the shore. "Have you got any fish?" he asked. The phrasing in the Greek implies a negative answer. It is like our saying to a sick person, "You are not well, are you?" or "You don't have the money for the hospital bill, do you?" So what Jesus really said was, "You did not catch anything, did you?" When he got the answer he expected, he told the little group to cast the net on the right side of the boat.

When they did, they got such a load of fish in the net that they could hardly haul it in. So the beloved disciple said to Peter, "That man must be the Lord."

Peter, who was stripped for working in the water, put on his fisherman's coat and started toward the Lord. They had caught 153 fish. Jerome believed that number significant, for that number represented all the varieties of fish in the whole of creation. Since the disciples are commissioned to fish for souls, symbolically the number stands for all the people in the world. The mission of the church is universal.

Jesus prepared breakfast for the lot. Once more, they had a fellowship meal together. This meal is reminiscent of the feeding of the five thousand around that same sea at the beginning of their association with Jesus.

As the others were doing various things, Jesus had a private conversation with Peter. He asked Peter if he loved him. Though Jesus uses the strong new gospel word for love *agape*, Peter in replying uses the more general weaker word *phileo*. At least this is the case for the first two questions. Both times Jesus asked, "Peter, do you love me?" He got back from Peter, "Yes, Lord, I have a friendly affection for you; I care for you." I guess Peter realized that in the light of his recent denial, he would not be sincere in saying more. The stronger word which he would like to use implies too much. It implies undying commitment. When Jesus got this weaker response twice from Peter, he, in the third question, uses the weaker word himself, as if to imply, "Peter, are you really sure you can go even this far and honestly say that you entertain a friendly feeling toward me and actually care for me?" Then it was, Peter said, "Lord, you know everything.

You know my real feelings toward you.'' Peter used the word *agape*.

The three times Peter denied Jesus have now been replaced by three affirmations. And the commission every time is ''Feed my sheep.'' In the Christian community, love invariably expresses itself in service. Love for the living Christ is shown by care for people in need. Christ can work and help them only through those who love him.

Yes, Jesus told Peter what his destiny was, that is, what his future would be. He was now in middle life. When he is old, he will be led where he does not want to go. Peter will end up in pagan Rome. Others will stretch out his arms for him. Jerome said, as do all the ancient exegetes and doctors of the church, that this means that Peter will be stretched out on a cross. Often exemplary discipleship eventuates in martyrdom.

When Peter looked around and saw that young disciple whom Jeses loved, he asked, ''Well, what about him? How will he fare?''

Jesus did not say, as many misunderstand him to say, ''This young man will live until I come again.'' All he said was, ''What business of yours is it if I should decide for this man to stay alive on earth until I come?'' His question is just that, a question, no more. It is intended as a rebuke.

Discipleship is individual and personal. It is adapted to the character and personality of the one who is called. It is not alike for everybody. Jesus taught with a gentle rebuke, ''You do your work, Peter; you carry out your assignment. Do not worry about anybody else. What I do with this young man is none of your business.''

John closes this epilogue, and with it his Gospel, by testifying that the beloved disciple, the very young man about whom Peter inquired, is the author of the Fourth Gospel. John affirms that his testimony is true. He knows it is true, because he has been an eyewitness to what he describes. Without penning his own name, it is obvious that he means the apostle John, the son of Zebedee, the disciple who leaned his head on the Master's breast at the Last Supper.

John is a consummate artist. His Gospel is almost perfect in design and arrangement. His prologue is one of the greatest pieces of theological literature ever penned. And his epilogue is the torch of responsibility and hope that Jesus himself passed on to his first disciples and through them to his followers in all ages. These resurrection appearances assign followers their responsibility and assure them of Jesus Christ's living and abiding presence that will afford them the power for its fulfillment.

QUESTIONS FOR REFLECTION AND STUDY

Introduction

1. Does it bother you that all four Gospels report different events in different ways?
2. Which of the four Gospel portraits of Jesus—the fulfillment of prophecy (Matthew); the active servant (Mark); God's message to all people, including the gentiles (Luke); or the incarnate God (John)—is most meaningful for you personally?

Chapter 1

1. "Jesus is the teacher who brings to life the truth which the Old Testament contains." What does Jesus help you to understand about the Old Testament? Does Jesus contradict your view of the Old Testament in any way?
2. "To all who received him, to them gave he power to become [children] of God." What does this verse imply about acknowledging Christ? What happens after a person recognizes who Christ is?
3. Why do you think the Virgin Birth is omitted from the Gospel which calls Jesus the incarnation of God?
4. "The mission of the Word...is both successful and unsuccessful, depending on the response it evokes." Is the validity of God's message proven only because and when people accept it? Is success having people agree with you?

Chapter 2

1. What is the reason for baptism today? How do infant and adult baptism differ?
2. "The gospel can't be used to dispossess the rich." Compare this statement with Luke 4:18–19, Matthew 19:16–24 and 6:19–21. Do the poor seem to have a favored place with Jesus? Do they have a special place with us?
3. "Segregation is anachronism." Is your church inclusive? Or does its membership mirror only one ethnic, socio-economic, or age group? Does its leadership mirror only one? What goals would be Christlike?
4. Do you initiate conversations about God, as Jesus did with the woman at the well? Can you think of ways to introduce the subject naturally?
5. Who are your enemies? Can you pray for them? Write a prayer for someone who dislikes you.

Chapter 3

1. Do you believe God still heals directly? Do you pray for physical healing for people who are ill?

2. Jesus' hearers had trouble making the shift from his talk about literal bread to his statements about the bread of heaven. He said some followed him only because there was something in it for them, either healing or food. Do we still get distracted from spiritual things by ''fringe benefits''? Name some.

3. What are your ''five loaves and two fishes''—what do you offer to Jesus to help meet others' needs?

4. Jesus offended the Jews' sensibilities with his talk about being bread and drinking blood. Even some of the disciples said, ''This is a hard saying; who can listen to it? (6:60, RSV) What teachings of Jesus are ''too hard'' for you?

5. Consider the woman taken in adultery. What sins do we exclude people for now?

Chapter 4

1. ''The truth shall set you free—but first it will make you miserable,'' says a Christian poster (it is a picture of a rag doll halfway through a set of wringers). Have you ever had an experience where it was painful to face and obey the truth? In what ways does facing the truth about life and ourselves set us free?
2. The disciples blamed the blind man's blindness on sin. In what ways do we still blame suffering people for their suffering?
3. The Pharisees were concerned about Jesus' *not* keeping the sabbath. What value is there in keeping the sabbath? Do you observe the sabbath?
4. How do you think we come to know God's voice, as the sheep know their shepherd's voice? How does God communicate with you, and how do you know it is God speaking?

Chapter 5

1. Jesus' words to the Jews about not believing in him come down hard on doubters. Does this seem to fit in with how Jesus usually dealt with people? Why do you think his words were so harsh in this instance?
2. "Jesus would give himself up in order to build the kingdom in the hearts of believers." What have you given up to build the kingdom in believers? What are you unwilling to give up?
3. Jesus said those who walk in the light do not stumble. If walking in the light means walking in God's way, with God's guidance, how do we explain the serious mistakes (stumblings) of committed believers?
4. Jesus and Lazarus' sisters wept and showed their grief. When Christians die, family members who are self-controlled and show no obvious grief are sometimes praised as strong and a people of exceptionally strong faith. What do you suppose are the assumptions behind such thinking?
5. List the miracles reported so far in this Gospel. How do the works of Jesus reported here compare to what believers do now? Are we and our churches involved in meeting the same sorts of needs that Jesus was? Which kinds of outreach do we avoid?

Chapter 6

1. The acts of homage done by Mary and those in the crowds were a way of recognizing him as Messiah. What acts of homage are meaningful to you as a modern person?
2. Some of those in authority (12:42–43) wanted to listen to Jesus and follow him, but that would have meant political trouble. How does this compare to public officials acknowledging Jesus now? Is Christianity a political asset or a liability? How do you respond to celebrities talking about their faith publicly?
3. Jesus assumed the role of a servant. How do you follow his example of personal service?
4. How do you feel when you hear the story of Peter's denying Jesus? Have you ever failed a friend publicly? How did you feel? How did you go about being reconciled?
5. Have you ever felt betrayed? How can you forgive someone who has deliberately done something to harm you?

Chapter 7

1. "The ultimate proof of Christianity lies in what it does." How do you respond to that assertion? Is Christianity something that can be proven?
2. Do you agree that the Holy Spirit segregates believers from non-believers? If so, in what ways? Does God's activity in our lives cause division? Is that God's intent, or is it caused by our response?
3. If showing love is how we win others to Christ, why will others reject and persecute us?
4. What phrase from Jesus' high priestly prayer evokes a strong response in you? Why?
5. Jesus asks God to keep believers in unity. In what ways has this prayer been answered? In what ways has it not been answered? What helps us toward unity? What hinders it?

Chapter 8

1. Peter did not want Jesus to submit to the authorities without a fight. When is it right to resist those in power? When is it wrong?
2. Pilate tried both to save Jesus' life and satisfy the demands of the crowd. How do you mediate conflicting demands in your life? What standards guide you in such situations?
3. What do you think enabled Jesus to remain calm during the ordeal of the trial? Are you able to remain calm in tough situations? What can we do in such times that Jesus did?
4. Jesus appeared to Thomas specifically to reassure him. Do we put forth a special effort to accept and reassure doubters? How do you respond to others' doubts? How do you respond to your own doubts?

Chapter 9

1. The disciples apparently went back to their old occupations after Jesus' death and resurrection. Why do you suppose they disbanded the group?
2. Jesus gave Peter an opportunity to cancel out each of his denials, asking him three times, "Do you love me?" How has God allowed you to cancel out some of your failures? Have you experienced the feeling of being forgiven for them?
3. What do you do to "feed God's sheep"?
4. If you were to write a gospel, telling God's good news, what acts of God that you have personally witnessed would you include to teach others about God's nature and activity?

About the Author

William R. Cannon received the Ph.D. degree from Yale University and has been awarded a number of honorary degrees. He began his ministry with pastorates in Georgia and joined the faculty of Candler School of Theology, Emory University, in Atlanta, in 1943, where he served as Dean for fifteen years prior to being elected to the episcopacy in 1968. Bishop Cannon presided over the Raleigh, Richmond, and Atlanta Episcopal Areas of the United Methodist Church until his retirement from episcopal supervision and administration in 1984.

Bishop Cannon, who now resides in Atlanta, describes himself as an inveterate traveler. He has made more than eighty trips abroad, many of them to the Holy Land, where he studied at the Jerusalem Center for Biblical Studies.

The Gospel of John is a companion volume to three previous commentaries by Bishop Cannon, *A Disciple's Profile of Jesus* on Luke, *Jesus the Servant* on Mark, and *The Gospel of Matthew,* all published by The Upper Room.